Percy Lifar

Other Ziggurat Books by
Marcus Reichert

Lost Lake: Early Poems
Confessions: Poems
Hoboken: A Novel
Art & Ego: Marcus Reichert
in Conversation with Edward Rozzo
Displaced Person:
Poetry, Pornography and Politics
(Selected Writings 1970-2005)

Percy Lifar

A Play
by
Marcus Reichert

*Introduction
by
Mel Churcher*

ZIGGURAT BOOKS
International

Percy Lifar
Copyright © 1986, 2012 by Marcus Reichert
Tenderly Remembered: An Introduction
Copyright © 2012 by Mel Churcher

All rights reserved. Except for brief passages quoted in
a newspaper, magazine, radio, or television program, no
part of this book may be reproduced in any form or by any
means, electronic or mechanical, including photocopying
and recording, or by any information storage and retrieval
system, without permission in writing from the Publisher.

Caution: This play is fully protected, in whole, in part, or in
any form under the copyright laws of the United States of
America, the British Empire including the Dominion of Canada,
and all other countries of the Copyright Union, and is subject
to royalty. All rights, including professional, amateur, motion
picture, radio, television, recitation, public reading, and any
method of photographic reproduction, are strictly reserved.

All enquiries concerning amateur and professional performing
rights should be addressed to Ziggurat Books International,
Editorial Office, 6 rue Argenterie, 30170 St. Hippolyte dy Fort,
France. – Enquiries: zigguratbooks@orange.fr

Front cover inset:
Boy 2012, painting by Marcus Reichert
Background image:
Water colour by Ryl Norquist

UK office:
27 St. Quentin House,
Fitzhugh Grove,
London SW18 3SE,
England

Printed in England by Imprint Academic
Seychelles Farm, Upton Pyne, Exeter, Devon EX5 5HY

Distributed by Central Books Ltd.
99 Wallis Road, London E9 5LN, England
Tel UK: 0845 458 9911
Fax UK: 0845 459 9912
Tel International: +44 20 8525 8800
Fax International: +44 20 8525 8879
E-mail: orders@centralbooks.com

First Edition

ISBN 978-0-9566579-9-2

Marcus Reichert is a painter and a poet who has also worked in film. His film works are held in the Archive of the Museum of Modern Art, New York. His Crucifixion paintings have been described by Richard Harries, the Bishop of Oxford, as being among the most disturbing painted in the 20th Century. Marcus Reichert lives and works in the south of France.

Mel Churcher is an actor and international voice and acting coach. As an actor, her work has included leading roles with the National Theatre and New Shakespeare Company, as well as television series including 'Upstairs, Downstairs'. She was voice and text coach for The RSC, Shakespeare's Globe, The Young Vic, The Royal Court and Regents Park Open Air Theatre and has coached on more than fifty major feature films. Mel Churcher is author of two books: *Acting for Film: Truth 24 Times a Second* (Virgin Books, 2003) and *A Screen Acting Workshop with DVD* (Nick Hern Books, 2011).

Percy Lifar (bearing the title Tenderly) was first performed by the Hot Toddy Theatre Company, with Mark Normandy directing, at the The Photographers' Gallery, London on 26th April 1987. Nick Hawker designed the set and Paul Holder created the sound.

Contents

Tenderly Remember: An Introduction by Mel Churcher	13
Act One	21
Act Two	57
Coda	97

Introduction

Tenderly Remembered
by Mel Churcher

It is 1986. The Chernobyl nuclear plant has exploded. Mrs Thatcher, who has broken the unions over the miners' strike, now allows US warplanes to mount attacks on Libya from British bases.

I, on the other hand, am concentrating on holding an umbrella over my head to protect myself from the radioactive rain, whilst combining mothering a seven year old and working as an actor. Out of the blue, I am asked to be in a new play by Marcus Reichert. It is to be directed by Mark Normandy and performed at The Photographers' Gallery in London's Covent Garden area. This is a most prestigious and unusual location.

The play, too, has an unusual and, possibly, prestigious location: The Edenbourne Asylum. It is a haunting place of dreams and hallucinations; of hopes and failures. It is a place of possibilities – its strange inhabitants destined to live endlessly meshed in each other's desires and fantasies, in an echo of Jean-Paul Sartre's 'Huis Clos'...

This densely written play depicts a dark, savage, absurd, yet comic and tender, world. We, the cast, are daunted, but excited. I am to play the small part of Mrs. Piper, an overripe matron, who feels she is forever young. She deals with loss by flirting outrageously with the hero of the piece, Percy Lifar (played by the actor, Ray Armstrong) who is trying to pick his way through an impenetrable briar of lost memory, with the help of his strange inmates.

I am of an age now that my memory has become a clutter of vivid snapshots rather than playing like a linear movie, and so I can only share a few of the images from that time:

We rehearsed in an old hospital or maybe it was a school. It was the holidays and my son came with me. I was terrified that the crumbling ceiling was full of asbestos. Looking back, I think it was not, but that the paranoia of this strange world we were inhabiting leaked out into my own world.

I look at my script now, full of my scribblings about what I – as my could-have-been self – wanted. What had led to my unresolved maternal longings? How was I to draw Percy to my breast? What could satiate my unfathomable desires? I see the world of this institution only through the eyes of Mrs Piper – Mrs Piper, who cannot conceive of a past; who probably cannot conceive. She sprays her cheap perfume and dreams of her Parisian music halls...

I endlessly asked about what I was to wear. My director didn't think it was important, but to me it was. I had played younger parts than myself all my career and now was being asked to play older; to play the very self that I might become – 'What ever happened to Baby Jane?' (An original photograph of Bette Davis, near the end of her career, now hangs in my hall. A friend asked the other day if the picture was of me...)

So I searched London for the right sixties clothes, the right wig and the right flower to wear at my breast. The flower that had become the essence of the child Mrs Piper may or may not have. The child that Percy – her Pierre – may or may not have fathered in her fancy's fancy with his insistent tickling stamen. I think I found it, the silk iris, in Liberty's. Iris was my mother's name (she died the following year).

Parents and children crop up a lot in this play. The roles we play. The tugs of love we may or may not experience. Relationships.

This world within the institution obeys its own surreal laws. It has it its own logic. It is peopled by those who believe; believe they may be great, and once cherubic, violinists or Christ-like figures who must assuage their guilt by crucifixion or that they must become the parents or children that they've never been. They may or may not be made to suffer the diabolical tortures that Percy describes to Mrs Piper, but they do suffer in their metaphorical imaginations. Dr. Lustig (played by the late lamented Peter Porteous) is the conduit to their dreams and nightmares.

The physical space of the Photographers Gallery has merged in my memory with the imagined world of the institution. I remember walls of glass, stairs that climbed steeply to a dark space of giant shadows thrown onto white walls. But whether these images were true or in my mind, I have no way of knowing now, as the gallery left its old home and moved to Soho in 2009.

Sartre wrote, 'Man first of all exists, encounters himself, surges up in the world – and defines himself afterwards.' This play is full of roles encountering themselves, and others, without being able to define themselves, or decide how they should proceed. They are defined only by their actions, but these are driven by whatever image they see of themselves at that moment in time. They act and react as actors do. For we are, after all, all actors playing on the world's stage. (Shakespeare said it better.)

I would not dare to say what the play is about but, for me, it examines the nature of reality and truth. Anything is possible. The author quotes Oscar Wilde in his superscription, 'The Universe itself shall be our immortality.'

Is it enough to believe something for it to be so? Well, after all, that's what actors do all the time. That is probably what sincere politicians do. And if they make it up and believe it, then, as the ageless Miss Ezrad says, 'Nobody will ever know the difference...They only know what they are told.'

And that is true for every part of our lives. This play, as metaphor, is truer now than it has ever been. We only know what we are told. And writers and artists, too, can tell us things. They are the dream weavers. And they can ask us questions, 'Do you dare to hear this story?' 'Whose story is it?'

And then they ask, as Percy asks, and as we all ask, 'Do you believe me?'

The Characters:

PERCY LIFAR

NURSE LATHROP

SISTER DANZELL

OSCAR BRUNO

DR. LUSTIG

TYRONE

VERA

RAY

MRS. PIPER

MR. PIPER

MISS EZRAD

Act One

Setting:

EDENBOURNE ASYLUM, EARLY SPRING

A section of the asylum: a grand staircase from the lobby to the floor above, which comprises a room with a bed, a chair, and a window, and a bit of hallway between the room and a balcony, which overlooks a paved promenade to the main gate. The promenade and gate remain unseen. Beyond the window of the room is a shaftway, which undergoes various transformations throughout the play. The shaftway is however usually defined only by darkness and light, so that the afore-mentioned transformations have the required impact.

Act One

SCENE 1

PERCY LIFAR *sits on the chair in his room. He is dressed in a white cotton shift. A light gauze covers his eyes and his hands are bandaged. It is difficult to say just how old* PERCY *is, maybe thirty, maybe forty or fifty, maybe even sixty. But it is clear that he has been kept from the world for a very long time: his paleness is indeed otherworldly. The shaftway is dressed as a shower-room, tiled and stark with shower-heads in a row.*

PERCY *sits, unmoving, for a long moment before* NURSE LATHROP *and* SISTER DANZELL *come in to attend to him.* LATHROP, *in her forties, is large and firm, while* SISTER DANZELL *is willowy, ineffectually so, and in her late thirties.* SISTER DANZELL *holds the tray as* NURSE LATHROP *prepares a new dressing for* PERCY'S *eyes. When* PERCY *speaks it's as if* NURSE LATHROP *and* SISTER DANZELL *weren't there. He speaks in a monotone.*

PERCY: Autobahn, autobiography, autocade, autocephalous ...

DANZELL: Do you think he can hear himself?

LATHROP: I really couldn't say, Sister.

DANZELL: Most likely he can.

PERCY: Avalanche, avant-garde, avarice, avatar, aventail, average, aversion – aversion – aversion – av – av – av –

DANZELL: (*Helpfully.*) Try aviary! (*He thinks her suggestion over.*)

PERCY: Aviary, aviation, aviator ...

(NURSE LATHROP *blocks* PERCY *from view as she examines his eyes. She steps back with a start.*)

PERCY LIFAR

LATHROP: Sister Danzell, he's opened his eyes!

DANZELL: Oh, isn't that wonderful, Nurse Lathrop! Isn't that wonderful!

LATHROP: We don't know if it's wonderful or not. I'll have to confer with Dr. Lustig on just how wonderful it is. Most likely, it is wonderful, but we can't be sure – we don't have all the details to hand.

(SISTER DANZELL *quietens herself, readily accepting her superior's judgement.*)

I think a slightly heavier bandage might be best until we've cleared the opening of the eyes with Lustig.

(*She sets about putting on a heavier bandage as* SISTER DANZELL *observes.*)

PERCY: Axlebox, axlepin, axletree, axolotl ...

(*He begins to fidget as the binding of his head continues. His monotone turns feverish and the words leave him more hastily, as if he were trying to hurry* NURSE LATHROP *in her work.*)

Azalea, azimuth, azurite – azurite – azurite –

DANZELL: If I'm correct, he's just finished with the AZ's ...

LATHROP: What a pity, he's becoming agitated.

DANZELL: (*Sincerely.*) What a pity.

LATHROP: Put that tray on the bed there and prepare to fix him.

ACT ONE

(SISTER DANZELL *dreamily sets the tray on the bed. As though she's forgotten where she is and what she's meant to be doing, she begins playing with the articles on the tray.*)

DANZELL: (*To herself.*) Such a pretty little tray. And such pretty little vials too, all sparkly with morning dew. Three clever syringes ... one, two, three. And cotton swabs as well, like little bunny-rabbits' tails –

LATHROP: Here, Sister, bring me Number One.

(*She injects* PERCY *with sedative.*)

And now Number Two ...

DANZELL: Vitamins, to keep him going.

LATHROP: And Three ...

DANZELL: The 'mystery cure': Number Three's good for whatever ails you.

LATHROP: (*Flirtatiously.*) That's right, Danzell, maybe you should try it sometime ...

DANZELL: (*Flattered, giggling.*) Oh, Nurse Lathrop, you're such a tease!

(NURSE LATHROP *casts an appraising eye on* SISTER DANZELL, *which causes her to blush deeply.* NURSE LATHROP *now confronts* PERCY, *having resumed her authoritarian deportment.*)

LATHROP: This man – (*examines the name-tag on his wrist*) P. Lifar – is fit to bathe with the others today. Prepare him for bathing!

PERCY LIFAR

DANZELL: Shall we forego the examination of his wounds then, Nurse Lathrop?

LATHROP: No, we shan't. I was getting to that.

(She proceeds to poke about his hands and chest with a long blunt metal instrument. PERCY obviously doesn't like this but the sedative is taking effect and each monotonal word comes more slowly now.)

PERCY: Baby, baby-farmer, babyhood, baby-sitter, baby-snatcher, baby-talk ...

DANZELL: *(Referring to his choice of words.)* That's nice.

LATHROP: *(Examining his hands.)* It's terrible what fire can do. It simply cooks the flesh, as if it were the Sunday joint. They're still rather bubbly and pink. A bit sore, I suspect. A little soap and water certainly can't make it any worse. *(Examining his chest-wound.)* And this is really just a streak now – not a scar as such – but really just the finest amount of oozing, but that's really only at one end, just below the sternum. I say he's fit to bathe! Get a robe on him, Sister! I'll check my roster for a suitable bathing partner!

(She goes into the hallway to get her clip-board. SISTER DANZELL helps PERCY to his feet, then searches the room for his robe, as he's left tilting drunkenly ... She finds the robe just as NURSE LATHROP re-enters the room.)

Quickly now, get that on him: they'll be coming by in a matter of minutes.

(They get the robe on him, sit him back down, and wait.)
OSCAR BRUNO, *a tiny old man with a wizened, smiling face and a bald head, appears at the end of the hallway. He finds his way to* PERCY's *room by reading the numbers above the doors. Sunlight streams cheerfully*

ACT ONE

from the tall windows above the stairwell down into the lobby. He and PERCY *will make their way down the stairs, through the lobby, and to the shower-room.*

(NURSE LATHROP *hears* OSCAR *coming, gets* PERCY *to his feet, and thrusts him into the hallway.* OSCAR *speaks with a chilling sweetness and an indistinct eastern European accent. He is terribly temperamental.*)

LATHROP: You are Oscar Bruno?

OSCAR: What a question! I'm the world's premier violinist – everybody knows that!

LATHROP: This man isn't blind but I'm entrusting him to you anyway. Take care he doesn't slip on anything. Very well then, off you go to the showers.

OSCAR: (*Taking hold of* PERCY.) Let go, I've got him!

LATHROP: (*Turning to* SISTER DANZELL *after they've left.*) What a character!

(NURSE LATHROP *and* SISTER DANZELL *exit, retracing* OSCAR's *path back along the hallway. At the top of the grand staircase, in a haze of sunlight,* OSCAR *stops to read* PERCY's *name-tag.*)

OSCAR: P. Lifar ... P. LIFAR?! (*Bursts out laughing.*) What on earth is P. Lifar?! Nobody's called P. Lifar!

PERCY: (*Wanting to explain.*) Backlog, back-number, backpedal ...

OSCAR: So you can talk! You are a poet? I am a world-famous violinist. And a nice man too.

PERCY LIFAR

(*They begin down the steps.*)

You can't see me but I'm very pretty too – I was a beautiful child. I had long golden hair and a mouth like a rosebud. I have a photograph. With all those bandages you'll have to take my word for it: I was a beautiful child. I was a prodigy too! This is rare, to have both – in such abundance. I am a wunderkind. So I hope you are honoured to be bathing with me. I don't know why they call it 'bathing', it's only a shower-room. I wish you could see me – I have eyes as big as bowls of black caviar. I have big, round eyes. Imploring eyes. Do you know what this means – 'imploring eyes'? I think not. 'Imploring eyes' are ghastly ... just ghastly ... and I have to have them, these big, round – sad – 'imploring eyes' ... (*Shudders at the thought.*)

(*They shuffle through the lobby,* OSCAR *guiding* PERCY *as they go.* OSCAR *can no longer resist telling* PERCY *the institution's darkest secret.*)

You don't know, not yet, but it's an epidemic of venereal disease – due to the excesses of the young soldiers gone off to war in Europe – filthy place – and returned home to further excesses. This hospice is falsely sanctioned – a quarantine centre for these young persons, the unsuspecting – like yourself, Lifar. They have flocked here – these young persons. (*Becoming over-excited.*) But it's no sanctuary! It's a guard-dogged oasis of perverted pleasure for the world's higher echelons! (*Gets a grip on himself.*) The detestable rich – who are falling apart – are caddied in here on rickshaws – through the tunnels – by Orientals. Said Orientals – who bow and suck their lips (*Demonstrates.*) in the most disgusting manner – are the only decent people in here – at the mineral salts spa – because that is precisely what this place is, P Lifar – (*Cackles.*) – a mineral salts spa! (*Cackles some more.*)

PERCY: (*Wanting to respond.*) Box-kite, box-office, box-tree ...

ACT ONE

OSCAR: Yes, a poet. I think we will get along splendidly.

(*They pause on the threshold to the shower-room. The room is empty, and echoey, and doesn't look like it's been used for ages.* OSCAR *sniffs, then grimaces.*)

Beguiling scents ... (*Sniffs again.*) Beguiling scents – hanging in the air. Smell 'em? From those atomizer things! (*Referring to the shower-heads.*)

(PERCY *swivels his round, in an upward movement, sniffing himself, feeling the gloom through his bandaged eyes.*)

A special occasion no doubt. (*Disdainfully.*) The grand viceroys love these special occasions. Any excuse to defile our young in vast numbers! Beguiling scents ... the last time I came here there were these cheap beguiling scents ... (*Takes a look around, suddenly shrieks, terrifying* PERCY.) Holy Mother of God, they've already been here!

(*But the room is empty as before.*)

There's no sign of life, Lifar – feel that? – it's as cold as a mortuary in here – as cold as a mortuary. Oh no, they haven't put the corpses away – they've just left them out – after playing with them! At least, you'd think, they could put them away! Maybe these Orientals are on holiday ... It's too bad you can't see how big this pile of young bodies is – it's pretty big – more than a dozen – and they're all naked. A military look to them too. Naked soldiers, I'd say ... (*Savours this image.*) Just a big pile of naked young men soldiers. What a mess. I hope you are thankful you can't see.

PERCY: (*Stammers in response.*) Ca-ca-cashbook, ca-ca-cashew, ca-ca-cashier, ca-ca-cashmere ...

PERCY LIFAR

(OSCAR *presses himself firmly to* PERCY, *as a frightened child would to its mother.*)

OSCAR: (*Hoarsely.*) Are you on their list, P Lifar? There must be a list. Do you think I'm on it too – or am I too old? You don't think I'm too old to be on the list, do you? (*Reaches under* PERCY's *shift to fondle him.*) I'm not too old, am I? What do you think? Who controls it anyway, their filthy list?! A moron I suppose, like Dr. Lustig – a moron who just doesn't know about things. (*Pleading.*) Isn't that so? Isn't that so, P. Lifar?! (*Shouts, angry that* PERCY *isn't responding to his caresses.*) Well, isn't it?!!

(NURSE LATHROP *and* SISTER DANZELL, *having heard* OSCAR *shout, tear along the hallway, down the grand staircase, across the lobby, and to the shower-room.* OSCAR *snatches up* PERCY's *wrist, then immediately throws it down.*)

P. LIFAR! PIFFLE! To die an untimely death is one thing, but to die an untimely death with a name like this?! Tell me – P. LIFAR – about this list – Who scribbles the names? – Who rubs them out?!

LATHROP: (*Arrested by* OSCAR's *shocking behaviour.*) What the devil! Danzell, let's get them apart!

OSCAR: It's only me, P. Lifar – only poor old Oscar with his ghastly imploring eyes ...

(NURSE LATHROP *and* SISTER DANZELL *take him away, abandoning* PERCY *to the dreadful scene* OSCAR *has described.*)

What ever became of that lovely little boy – a genius – a genius, I tell you – with his beautiful blonde hair – and his little lips – like the petals of a rosebud!

ACT ONE

(In the lobby, NURSE LATHROP *and* SISTER DANZELL *give* OSCAR *over to* DR. LUSTIG, *who patiently leads him off.* NURSE LATHROP *and* SISTER DANZELL *stroll back to see what's become of* PERCY.)

LATHROP: Men ...

DANZELL: Really, for heaven's sake.

(They pause before entering the shower-room, just in case PERCY *might be violent too. He is trying to control his trembling. Hesitantly – because he doesn't know what awaits him – he unravels the long bandage about his head and lets it drop snaking to the shower-room floor.* NURSE LATHROP *and* SISTER DANZELL *find this fascinating and make no move to stop him. Finally, his eyes now revealed. He opens them, and casts a slow glance over the scene, lastly stopping on* NURSE LATHROP *and* SISTER DANZELL.)

PERCY: *(In altogether succinct and commanding tones.)* I TOO WOULD BE THE SUBLIMEST OF CHARACTERS IF ONLY I HAD A STORY TO TELL!

(NURSE LATHROP *stares blankly at* SISTER DANZELL, *who stares blankly back.*)

LATHROP: First complete sentence – must make a note of it for Dr. Lustig.

DANZELL: Some sentence.

Darkness.

SCENE 2

PERCY *and* DR. LUSTIG *are sitting on the balcony. It is a pleasant day and they are taking the air,* PERCY *wrapped in a heavy robe and* DR.

PERCY LIFAR

LUSTIG *in the usual white smock.* DR. LUSTIG *is nondescript, but godlike. We have joined them at a hiatus in their conversation.*

DR. LUSTIG: Now do you understand why they've brought you here ... ?

PERCY: (*Repeating what he's already been told.*) Oscar Bruno's fondness for me was developing into something akin to pain – or before that?

DR. LUSTIG: Mr Bruno was obliged to assume the role of your guardian. Mr. Bruno feared the very air he breathed.

PERCY: Oh.

(DR. LUSTIG *realizes he's getting nowhere.*)

DR. LUSTIG: I see here (*referring to his clip-board*) the nurses have removed your stitches – very good, very good indeed. And, let's see ... (*Examines PERCY's hands.*) Yes, your hands are very nearly healed too. Nurse Lathrop tells me you've asked for pen and paper ... perhaps you'd like to write to someone?

PERCY: No. (*Here follows a veil of lies.*) It's just there are certain things which have occurred to me recently that I'd like to put down, things of such a delicate nature, in the overall scheme of things, that I could easily allow to drown as my mind becomes inundated with more mundane and brutal matters.

DR. LUSTIG: 'Mundane and brutal matters.'

PERCY: **Mundane and brutal** in a manner of speaking. You see, my mind is presently in a state of agitation, and although my thoughts are confused, misshapen even, they are pure, and delicate ...

ACT ONE

DR. LUSTIG: Yes, I know. Thoughts of such a fragile nature most often do fall prey to the coarseness of our daily lives, Mr. Lifar.

PERCY: But that's not my name. I don't know what my name is but it's not Lifar. I wouldn't have a name like Lifar, unless I was making a joke of some kind.

DR. LUSTIG: And why not? Isn't Lifar a perfectly good name?

PERCY: Hardly.

DR. LUSTIG: Oh?

PERCY: It doesn't mean anything Lifar. Not a thing. **Lifar's** the name of a ballet-dancer. How do I know? Because Oscar Bruno told me so. The ballet-dancer gave this name meaning, not the other way round. Imagine his entrance: he turns to the house and whispers 'Excuse this interruption, even before I've begun the ballet, but I can't see what **Lifar** has got to do with me; in fact, I resent the use of so meaningless and vulgar a word in relation to myself, or my dance ...' Then perhaps, if Lifar were lucky enough, some member of the audience still retaining his wits might call out 'What shall we call you then?' ... to which Lifar answers 'Why, just watch me dance and then decide!'

DR. LUSTIG: You're no relation to this dancer fellow then I take it?

PERCY: How should I know? (*Sighs.*) No. It's a lazy name for a lazy boy, a boy too lazy to think of an original name for himself. But I do have original thoughts, perishable however, unfortunately. That's why I'd like something to write with.

DR. LUSTIG: I'll see what I can do.

(*He rises.*)

PERCY LIFAR

PERCY: Please, Dr. Lustig. After all, this wing of Edenbourne does bear your name. Doesn't it?

DR. LUSTIG: (*Smiles broadly.*) That's what the sign says.

PERCY: Good.

DR. LUSTIG: Come along Mr. Lifar (*helping* PERCY *to his feet*), I'd say it's rather too chilly out here for you now.

PERCY: Why not call me **Percy**?

DR. LUSTIG: If you find it less formal ...

PERCY: Please. I do.

(*They move away from the parapet of the balcony toward the doors to the hallway, however* PERCY *chooses to linger awhile longer.*)

Dr. Lustig, there's a horse tied at the bottom of the shaftway outside my window. It whinnies and rears up, and stamps its hooves on the cobbles ... Horses are such valiant beasts, don't you think, with their big vulnerable noses?

DR. LUSTIG: You're mistaken: it's not a horse crying down there, it's a negro man named Tyrone.

(PERCY *finds this hard to believe.* DR. LUSTIG *leads* PERCY *to his room.* PERCY *goes in and sits on his bed.* DR. LUSTIG *locks the door behind him.* DR. LUSTIG *descends to the lobby and exits as daylight turns to dusk and night falls.* PERCY *turns to address an invisible listener, the audience.*)

PERCY: My room was whiter still in the moonlight, the shadows tense and crisp. Over the shaftway hung the moon like a shiny coin at the wrong end of a telescope and at the bottom of the

ACT ONE

shaftway, as usual, stood the horse. From the heavens fell a
silver cord upon which I was to descend. I didn't look into
the rooms I passed as I descended even though I was sorely
tempted. But I did hear strange sounds, stranger than those on
my floor. It was exceedingly dark where I was headed and all
I could see of Tyrone were his grimacing teeth and wide eyes.
He held his fists pressed to his temples (TYRONE *is now
illuminated where he stands in the shaftway*) like a man caught
in a gigantic ringing metal drum. But there was only the slight
whirring of a ventilating fan in a tiny tin box by his feet. (*This
sound.*) The big man reached up to help me the rest of the way
down. My feet touched earth. I offered my hand and his closed
round it.

(*PERCY goes to the window beyond which the silver cord is now
hanging. He grasps the cord and is lowered into the shaftway where
TYRONE awaits him. They shake hands as described.*)

I know: your name is Tyrone. And mine, as far as we know, is
P. Lifar. Percy. Lifar, same as the French ballet-dancer: it's one
of the few facts I have that I'm absolutely certain of, had it from
a good source, a distinguished violin player. Maybe you can
tell me, Tyrone: what's going on, not only here, inside, but
outside?

(TYRONE *looks curiously up at the moon. His hand alights on*
PERCY's *shoulder. He smiles.*)

TYRONE: I enjoy my chores ... more than anything else in this life.
The steam satisfies my soul, it lifts the crushing weight of my
sin on its dove-like wings.

PERCY: Aren't you the gentleman who bellows down here in the
dark every night, or nearly every night?

PERCY LIFAR

TYRONE: Indeed I am. But I'm also a trustee, and the man who feeds your dirty dishes into that steaming monster who passes wind through this duct. (*Points to the tiny box, which continues to softly whirr.*) I'm just waiting for my crucifixion. I'd like to die hanging on that wall ... (*Points to an expanse above them.*) That's where I see myself hanging, on the Cross of Jesus.

(*He stares beseechingly at the wall, admires an invisible TYRONE who already suffers there with dignity.*)

I'm going to have to escort you back upstairs, Mr. – ?

PERCY: Lifar.

(TYRONE *rises on his toes, stretches to an unearthly length, claws at the silvery dust surrounding the moon, and wails.*)

TYRONE: God help me!

PERCY: (*Wonderstruck.*) God help us all.

(TYRONE *resumes his normal size and smiles apologetically at* PERCY.)

What happened, Tyrone?

TYRONE: I killed my mother and father. And my sister, Paulita. I ran from the house with blood soaking my clothes. The night was cold and the blood froze. I killed my mother and father while they were sleeping. They were facing each other, like playing cards. I used two knives – from the kitchen. It was quicker that way. Paulita was in the doorway, watching – I didn't know she was there. And then I killed her. She was shivering – when I killed her. I cut her throat because I thought it would be quicker, but it wasn't. Then I tried to cut my own throat, but it hurt too much – I couldn't do it. I ran from the

ACT ONE

house soaking with blood carrying the two knives. You know, that blood was frozen all over me by the time they got me. I hit an artery in Paulita's neck. The neighbour's dog got his teeth into my trouser and wouldn't let go. I had to cut him up pretty bad. He made a terrible noise, there in the street, that dog. God help me.

PERCY: Some story.

TYRONE: I know. A whopper.

PERCY: I'll say.

TYRONE: Yea.

(*He gazes with some consternation at* PERCY.)

What happened to you? (*In a whisper.*) I've got the time, really, if you want to tell me ...

PERCY: It's rather boring I'm afraid.

TYRONE: (*Disappointed.*) Oh.

PERCY: It's worse than boring, Tyrone.

TYRONE: I'm sorry. We've all got our crosses to bear.

(*He gazes longingly at the wall.*)

PERCY: Maybe. My problem is I don't know why I should be carrying a cross – I haven't any story – except maybe Oscar Bruno ... (*Ponders this.*) No, Oscar doesn't count really: I met Oscar after I got here – er, there – after I woke up, I mean.

TYRONE: You were asleep?

35

PERCY LIFAR

PERCY: I was asleep for a long time. I guess.

TYRONE: (*Turning manic.*) Man has a no-good pathological side, you know. I avoid these evil cogitations by being in here.

PERCY: Is it worth avoiding though, Tyrone – you see, I don't know.

TYRONE: Worth avoiding, you say?! It's these electronic devices that have contributed to man's downfall. Contributed substantially. Electronic devices too numerous to tell – the devil's charity.

PERCY: Goodness.

TYRONE: Goodness, nothing. He possesses the human organism now – in all its variant forms. He's a greedy shopper, the devil. Buys up all the eggs you got: brown, white, yellow, even black, like me. He bought me – substituted an electronic device. That's why my soul is no good. An electronic device ... God help me! What can I say, Percy, it's true.

(*He shakes his head sadly, and tears come to streak his cheeks.*)

PERCY: Cheer up, Tyrone, at least you've got something to say for yourself. Consider me – what have you got? – a man with nothing to say for himself.

(TYRONE *thinks on this.*)

TYRONE: I'd say make something up but that would be lying and lying's a sin. Believe me, you don't want sin on your conscience. Believe me.

PERCY: You're probably right.

ACT ONE

TYRONE: I am. I know.

(TYRONE *sighs, wanders in a tight circle, like a dog trying to find a spot to lie down. He does, in shadow, not far from* PERCY's *feet.* PERCY *gazes down at him, liking him. Then he addresses his invisible listener.*)

PERCY: Tyrone's oily tears often anointed his dark cheeks as he thought on the grotesque event that had brought him there. His handsome face glistened like a well-polished gourd. Why befriend Tyrone?, you may ask. The answer is simple: I could learn from him. Tyrone talked and talked and talked – there in the shaftway – about his crime, about absolution and remission of sin, about crucifixion – his own, naturally – and about the heavenly kingdom, where the devil couldn't buy you off the shelf and replace your soul with an electronic device. Yes, indeed there was much to be learned from Tyrone –

(TYRONE *abruptly sits up, jettisoned from a dream.*)

TYRONE: Radioactive lice! There I was in the River Jordan, naked and innocent as the day I was born! Where does a man go to wash away the devil's work – radioactive lice, the devil's radioactive lice? Why, a man goes to the River Jordan! (*Stands, refers to his own physiognomy.*) The body of a true sinner! This body, a sinner's body! (*Begins taking off his white dishwasher's uniform.*) Naked and cleansed at last, but still the body of a sinner! God help me!
PERCY: Easy, Tyrone – you'll catch your death of cold down here with nothing on ...

(*He tries to restrain him but the bigger man lifts* PERCY *high in the air and holds him there.*)

My goodness.

PERCY LIFAR

TYRONE: Naked and cleansed at last – think of it, Percy! I once longed to bathe the dust from my Saviour's feet. But, you know, such a longing is a sin in itself! Do you know why, Percy, why such a longing is a sin?

PERCY: No.

TYRONE: Conceit! What vanity to think for a moment that I might be so blessed ...

(*He gently lowers* PERCY *to the ground.*)

Feeding the dishwasher has helped. It has allowed me to serve without those I serve knowing. So my task is a thankless one, as it should be, and therefore blessed.

PERCY: That's one way of looking at it.

TYRONE: I pray daily that it shall remain so, until that miracle – hopefully a faceless one – comes to lift me onto that cross.

(*Again he gazes up at the wall, and* PERCY's *gaze follows his. They remain that way for a long moment. Then comes the voice of an unexpected presence, impersonal, amplified and cold.*)

THE VOICE: Tyrone Powell, please report to your captain. Tyrone Powell, please report.

PERCY: Oh well.

TYRONE: Oh well.

(TYRONE *lifts* PERCY *up to the cord, which* PERCY *grasps. As he ascends,* TYRONE *watches from the bottom of the shaftway.*)

Fade out.

ACT ONE

SCENE 3

A long slant of afternoon light divides the lobby. VERA and RAY, plainly dressed, sit on one side while PERCY and DR. LUSTIG sit on the other. VERA and RAY remain unaware of their presence. VERA and RAY must be noticeably younger than PERCY.

DR. LUSTIG: Vera and Ray.

(PERCY *looks at them, then at* DR. LUSTIG, *not comprehending.*)

Vera and Ray, Percy, your mother and father.

PERCY: Mother and father?

DR. LUSTIG: Mother and father.

(VERA *and* RAY *stare steadfastly ahead. They slowly cross and uncross their legs. They are worried.*)

PERCY: This is news to me.

DR. LUSTIG: How's that, Percy?

PERCY: Well, I've never seen them before.

DR. LUSTIG: What do you make of them?

(PERCY *studies the two carefully.*)

PERCY: Uniformly peculiar people, I'd say ...

DR. LUSTIG: Why peculiar? I'd say they look perfectly normal.

PERCY: Oh.

PERCY LIFAR

DR. LUSTIG: Obviously you don't agree.

(PERCY *doesn't, but doesn't know quite what to say.*)

PERCY: Are they demonstration models, doctor?

DR. LUSTIG: (*Laughs.*) No, they're the real thing, an actual mother and father. They're interesting aren't they.

PERCY: I guess. They look as if their feet weigh a ton.

DR. LUSTIG: They've been worried about you.

(PERCY *continues to stare curiously at them.*)

PERCY: Pork chops.

DR. LUSTIG: What? How's that, Percy?

PERCY: Pork chops.

DR. LUSTIG: What about pork chops, is it coming back to you – is their presence bringing it back?

PERCY: No, I'm afraid not. It's just this fellow's hands make me think of pork chops – the way he's staring at them – like pork chops, like pork chops he can't quite bring himself to eat. Maybe he doesn't have much of an appetite right now.

DR. LUSTIG: I should think not: they've been terribly worried about you.

PERCY: Yes, but he's got to eat, this fellow – ?

DR. LUSTIG: Ray.

ACT ONE

PERCY: Right. This fellow Ray's got to eat.

DR. LUSTIG: I'm sure he does, Percy. I'm sure they both eat.

PERCY: That's a relief.

DR. LUSTIG: How's that?

PERCY: Well, they don't look like they eat. They look like they just sit.

DR. LUSTIG: It's only that they're sitting just now. They're waiting to see you.

PERCY: Me? Why me?

DR. LUSTIG: I've told you: they're your mother and father.

PERCY: I don't think so, doctor. No, I don't think they are actually.

DR. LUSTIG: They've come a long way, Percy. I can't just send them away. They want to see you, to visit with you. They want to try and help. Your solitude is an unhealthy one.

PERCY: Maybe, but I'd rather they came back in a week or so. Let them be re-absorbed by the sands of time for a little while longer.

DR. LUSTIG: Well, you're letting them down terribly.

PERCY   I am?

DR. LUSTIG: You are. Not a very charitable attitude, I'd say.

PERCY: But what's to give? – I haven't anything to give them.

PERCY LIFAR

DR. LUSTIG: Just to be with you after all this time will be enough. Believe me, it will.

(PERCY *observes* VERA *and* RAY *even more carefully.*)

PERCY: Look, Dr. Lustig, see what a mess she's made of her tissue – she's wrung the life out of it – there's nothing left – just a frayed bit of fluff. And he's filled that ashtray to the top – it's brimming with butts – not just two or three – like any normal person – but a few hundred maybe ...

(DR. LUSTIG *disapproves of such exaggeration.*)

Why, they're so wrought up they can't even speak. You see, nothing. Are their lips moving? No. Well, they're beyond speech, aren't they? How are they to speak to me if they can't speak to each other? They haven't anything to say for themselves. So what good are they to me? I need people who have something to say for themselves. Not nothing. Think about it, Dr. Lustig ... not nothing.

DR. LUSTIG: I can tell you, Percy, they have plenty to say for themselves.

PERCY: I was afraid of that.
DR. LUSTIG: Come along, Percy, let's see what they have to say for themselves. You might even like it.

PERCY: I doubt it.

DR. LUSTIG: Well, come along anyway, let's just see ...

(*As* PERCY *exits the lobby, by way of the staircase to the balcony above,* DR. LUSTIG *joins* VERA *and* RAY. *The long slant of afternoon light rises from the lobby floor to fall directly on* PERCY

ACT ONE

where he stands on the balcony. The lobby below is now in darkness.
PERCY *addresses his invisible listener.*)

PERCY: When Vera saw me her eyes glistened. They glistened with tears bright as seltzer. She and Ray stood in my doorway in silhouette. Ray looked me over and sighed. They were honest, caring people, Vera and Ray. They were concerned. It was their concern that terrified me most. They'd brought lunch. She had it in a brown paper bag. Everything: plates, knives, forks, glasses, spoons, food ... the works. I pretended to be asleep. Their lunch was singularly unappealing. Spam and cold boiled potatoes, I think. I was roused, my own lunch brought in on a tray as usual. Tomato soup – served in an old porcelain bowl with a yellow stripe round the edge. A crust lay over the soup. Under the crust was a watery orangish stuff. Not much taste. When it was broken the crust made a kind of filigree – ragged and drifting – steaming too, like cooling lava. A bit of parsley marked the centre of the soup – the approximate centre. The parsley came to be fastened more firmly in time and place as the broken crust cooled and thickened and clung to it. It seemed this bit of parsley exerted an uncanny centripetal force on the scum ...

(*He thinks on this for a moment.*)

During lunch they talked about religion. I hadn't detected any signs of religion at Edenbourne except for Tyrone. In essence, Vera believed we lived in a misbegotten world, that humans had tumbled through a crack in the floor – a crack in the floor in heaven, that is – and that us humans now stared draft-draft back up at this immense crack from whence we came. And of course the great question was: how to get back through the crack? Ray agreed that we all had to work very hard to reverse the crack-master's low opinion of us: if the crack-master hadn't had such a low opinion of us he wouldn't have booted us through the crack in the first place. Bit of logic there, I'd say.

PERCY LIFAR

As Vera had it, the crack-master had been reconsidering things for some time. And maybe he was just about to reach down and pluck us back up – back up through the crack. Once back up through the crack – why, we'd all be cradled in the heavenly light of the big room upstairs! It all sounded vaguely familiar but she went on at such length that I lost interest and did indeed fall asleep, and they left. But Vera and Ray came back the next day ... (*Nods in direction of his room, where* VERA *and* RAY *are now sitting by his empty bed eating lunch.*)

(PERCY *leaves the balcony and goes to his room. He gets into bed and* SISTER DANZELL *brings in a bowl of tomato soup for him. She smiles at* VERA *and* RAY *and leaves.* PERCY *pokes at his soup with his spoon, to break up the aforementioned crust.*)

VERA: You know, Preston, you were an unusually morose infant.

PERCY: Who, me?

VERA: He was wasn't he, Ray? (*Smiles lovingly at* PERCY.)

RAY: No bouncing babykins.

VERA: No, only gurgled when his darling little head was tucked in his darling little blanket. How you loved that raggedy ole 'ba' ...

RAY: Went wrong from the start, I'd say. And I still say it was that nasty circumcision –

VERA: Really, Ray!

RAY: Well, it was Preston got his willy nipped.

ACT ONE

VERA: Well, I know, but why bring it up now – we're having lunch. Isn't this fun, Preston, all of us having lunch together? And what a beautiful day for it. It is isn't it, Ray?

RAY: Couldn't be lovelier.

VERA: (*Laughs.*) That really was some day though, when – well, you know. Preston, your Aunt Evelyn didn't know what to do! What a kerfuffle! There we all were round your Aunt Evelyn's dining-room table – the whole family was on hand.

RAY: Yea, and that Reginald of yours was four sheets to the wind.

VERA: You know my brother can't stand the sight of blood! Imagine if you'd had your kitty run over right before your very eyes! And who are you to talk anyway – running for the plasters every time you nick yourself shaving!

RAY: Blood you gave 'em, eh, Pressers?! Well, boy, did you or did you not give 'em blood?!!

PERCY: Maybe that's why I developed an early fondness for adults in white.

RAY: I'm not sure I follow, son.

PERCY: Surely you remember how I used to walk up to perfect strangers in white at the seaside and put my little hand in theirs?

(*A flight of fancy.* VERA *and* RAY *glance at one another with dismay.*)

Well, I did, whether you remember it or not. I just slipped my little hand in theirs.

PERCY LIFAR

(PERCY *is enjoying himself.*)

VERA: But why? Why do such a thing, Preston?

PERCY: Because they were all doctors, as far as I was concerned, and doctors know how to cure what ails, don't they?

RAY: Good thinking, son.

VERA: (*Tittering.*) Why, yes, good thinking, son.

RAY: You should have been there, son – bloody hell, did you ever wriggle and squeal when they nipped your little dinger. Just like a little piglet. (*Laughs.*) It just wasn't on! And it wasn't so little either! Bloody hell, what a day that was, eh, Vera?!

VERA: No need to use bad language, Ray.

RAY: (*Quietening down.*) No, quite right, dearest.

VERA: You know, Preston, you did squirt quite a bit on your Aunt Evelyn's guests. And floods of tears.

RAY: What a boy – kid soaked half the towels in the house. What a day ...

VERA: What a day ...

PERCY: Night soil.

VERA: What's that, dear?

PERCY: Night soil – what I must have left in my nappy.

VERA: All babies do. No cause for being ashamed. All babies do.

ACT ONE

PERCY: Oh.

VERA: You know, Preston, daddy used to take you along in our old luncheon-basket when he went to work on the aeroplanes. Ray, where's that photograph of you and little Preston sitting on the wing?

RAY: Oh yea. Just a sec ... (*Begins searching his pockets for the photograph.*)

VERA: Well, where is it? You were meant to bring that photograph along to show the boy!

RAY: Just a sec, I said. Just a sec ...

(*But he can't find it.*)

PERCY: Forget it. How about an history of the world? You know, with ancient cities and the like ...

VERA: Well now, let me think. Ray, do we know any stories like that?

RAY: What, with ancient cities?

VERA: Yes, with ancient cities.

(RAY *searches his mind.*)

RAY: No, I don't personally. But maybe you do, dearest. Don't you?

VERA: I'm not sure I do actually.

PERCY: Oh well.

PERCY LIFAR

RAY: Sorry to disappoint you, son.

VERA: Maybe you'd like some pudding instead: I've made a lovely apple tart –

RAY: Why lie to the boy – you're setting a bad example.

(VERA *bursts into tears.*)

VERA: You know I can't bake worth nothing, so why shouldn't I buy it?! It's just not fair! And why bring it up in front of the boy, Ray? Why?

RAY: Because we agreed: no prevarications! And you were meant to stick by that!

(VERA *continues to weep and moan.* RAY *tries to comfort her but she's inconsolable.* VERA *slips from her chair onto the floor, where she kicks and shrieks like a spoiled child.*)

(*To* PERCY.) What do we do now?

PERCY: Is she often like this?

RAY: Afraid so. She's rather immature. But I love her.

PERCY: I guess that helps.

RAY: (*Philosophically.*) It does really. I don't know what I'd do if I didn't.

PERCY: Maybe I'd better ring for Nurse Lathrop.

RAY: That sounds a smashing idea.

(PERCY *does. The bell chimes angelically over* VERA's *moaning.*)

ACT ONE

Fade out.

SCENE 4

Twilight on the balcony. PERCY *and* DR. LUSTIG *are both sitting. A bleak night is blowing in and they occasionally shiver with the cold as they prolong their stay out-of-doors.*

PERCY: When I was born they looked at me and wept, or so they say. So why should they want to claim me as their own now? Really, doctor.

DR. LUSTIG: It's quite simple: mothers and fathers are like that. You're their progeny, their immortality, so to speak, as they see it, and they want you to have the best, and be the best.

PERCY: Rather ridiculous, wouldn't you say, considering my situation?

DR. LUSTIG: You've made progress. They've demanded more tests.

PERCY: But who are they to demand more tests?

DR. LUSTIG: Look here, Percy, they've demanded more tests, but there aren't any more tests to be given – unless we were to concoct a few. And they aren't coming back until more tests are given. So you've nothing to worry about – for the time being. How's that, feel better now?

PERCY: Not really. I mean, who are they to demand more tests?!

DR. LUSTIG: If you really want to know, they're paying the bills.

PERCY: Those two, paying my bills? But they can't even afford – well, I don't mean to be unkind ...

DR. LUSTIG: That's nice. You see, you are making progress.

PERCY: I find this very low comedy, Dr. Lustig, very low comedy indeed. You know, don't you?

DR. LUSTIG: No, I don't know. Know what?

PERCY: What? They: subjective. Them: objective. Theirs: possessive. That's really all there is to it.

DR. LUSTIG: In a manner of speaking, yes. But in the broader sense, no.

PERCY: It's a bordello.

DR. LUSTIG: How's that?

PERCY: It's a bordello, I said, this place is a bordello. Oscar was right.

DR. LUSTIG: What's that make me?

PERCY: Suit yourself.

DR. LUSTIG: Well now, that's not very nice.

PERCY: Hardly.

DR. LUSTIG: Now what have we done to deserve this?

PERCY: But, doctor, why me? Why foist me off on Vera and Ray? Why not Tyrone for instance?

DR. LUSTIG: That should be obvious.

PERCY: What? He's nearly as hirsute as I am!

ACT ONE

DR. LUSTIG: He may be nearly as hirsute as you are but he is the wrong colour.

PERCY: Not the right colour?! So what?! (*Cries out.*) Forgive me, Tyrone! Give 'em Tyrone anyway ... Give 'em Tyrone. And further more, doctor, they believe in the same things – Tyrone and Vera and Ray – they have religion! On second thought, don't give 'em Tyrone: I couldn't do that to such a – well, to someone so Christ like ...

DR. LUSTIG: That's very kind of you, Percy ---

PERCY: I thought I was supposed to be **Preston**?!

DR. LUSTIG: Confidentially, I like Percy better. But you'll have to get used to Preston. You're angry now, aren't you?

PERCY: You could say that.

(*They pass a long moment gazing out over the grounds of the institution.*)

DR. LUSTIG: (*Referring to the vine charcoal PERCY's been given to write with.*) You don't like this?

PERCY: It's unsuited for the job.

DR. LUSTIG: It would be unwise, wouldn't it, to give you a sharp implement just now ...

PERCY: Oh, would it? I wouldn't know.

DR. LUSTIG: Why not write something for me, something we could work with?

PERCY LIFAR

PERCY: If I were to write anything – of consequence – with this (*raises a fistful of charcoal*), I'd have to cover the walls with it – it's just too big! I can't **negotiate** the page with it, as they say.

DR. LUSTIG: As who says?

PERCY: Why, those who use such expressions – as **negotiate**, to **negotiate** this or that.

DR. LUSTIG: And who are they?

PERCY: I don't know – the higher echelons, I guess. The higher echelons of humankind. That sounds good.

DR. LUSTIG: And where did you pick up this expression: higher echelons?

(*PERCY things on this for a moment, then remembers.*)

PERCY: From Oscar Bruno ... Radioactive lice! A memory! A MEMORY OF MY OWN!

(*He leaps up, embraces* DR. LUSTIG, *drawing him to his feet, and dances him round the balcony as he sings.*)

A memory ... just a silly, sad old memory ... just a silly, sad old memory ... like dandruff on your shoulder, like a chair that you can fold, dear ... just a silly, sad old memory ...

DR. LUSTIG: Lovely rhythm.

PERCY: Thank you.

DR. LUSTIG: Alright now, enough fun for the moment. Perhaps we should just wait and see – I mean about the pen.

ACT ONE

PERCY: (*Releasing* DR. LUSTIG.) Enough fun for the moment then.

DR. LUSTIG: I think so, but we'll see about that pen ...
(*Again they sit.* PERCY *stares off.*)

Do you really think your hands are well enough to make such exacting marks? Drawing is one thing but writing is another. Percy?

(*He observes* PERCY's *sudden self-absorbed state, makes a note.*)

Why don't we have a go at some free-association ...

(*He checks his watch.*)

Fine, we've just enough time before your next injection. Now, how about a bit of free-association before your nap?

(PERCY *turns to gaze at him without interest.*)

The birds clustered in the uppermost branches of that tree? That one – yes, way over there beyond the steeple ...

(*They both peer into the distance.*)

PERCY: Blackbirds, sniplets of black cut from a piece of black paper. And the branches, a dingy ruffle of lace. I don't know. What about those heavy clouds, are they saying something too? Or am I presupposing too much?

DR. LUSTIG: No, that's how it works. Analogies can be very helpful: the deeper you delve into your imagination – to associate, to compare – the deeper, simultaneously, you're delving into your memory. The very texture of your sensibility is manifest in this way. So, what about those heavy clouds?

Your use of the word **heavy** is interesting – most people think of clouds as light, and airy. You see ...

PERCY: I also see that roll of clouds as a wave curling back on itself, so that now the birds and branches make a fan, a delicate fan hovering before the wave, almost as it it's being held closer to us, by an invisible hand, and the hand is about to cast the fan into the sea. But it's a picture, fixed, and the fan will always be there, hovering before the wave, like that.

DR. LUSTIG: But the wave won't. As you can see, it's dispersing at this very moment. It's moving off to the east.

PERCY: There, the birds have flown now too.

(*They watch as the birds fly away.*)

Curtain.

Act Two

Act Two

SCENE 1

MRS. PIPER *and* PERCY *sit in the lobby. She is in her forties and behaves in a girlish manner that is unflattering for a woman her age. Her suit fits too tightly and her wig is a garish shade of orange.* PERCY *is fascinated by her. Nurses and orderlies occasionally pass by.*

PERCY: My baby?! But how can this be, I've never seen you before!

MRS. PIPER: Do you like my flower?

> (*She thrusts her breast forward, the flower pinned there leaping at* PERCY.)

I wore it especially for you. It's an iris – your favourite ---

PERCY: My favourite? Irises?

MRS. PIPER: (*Blushing.*) You tickled my fancy with one that very night –

PERCY: What very night?

MRS. PIPER: (*Blushing more deeply.*) The night you impregnated me –

PERCY: Impregnated who?!

MRS. PIPER: Why me, silly, that's why we're having a baby –

PERCY: But I'm not having a baby!

MRS. PIPER: Of course not, we're having it together. I'm the mommy and you're the daddy. That's how it's done, silly.

PERCY: I wish you wouldn't call me that.

MRS. PIPER: (*Indignantly.*) Well, you never minded before. You didn't mind being called – that – when I was tickling **your** fancy, did you? No, I guess not. You liked it fine then, didn't you? I wish we could do that some more right now!

(*She throws her arms round him.*)

PERCY: Easy, lady – I don't know what you're talking about!

MRS. PIPER: (*Giggling.*) Oh yes you do. That's how we did it, remember? You put your fancy in my fancy and –

PERCY: Please, you're making me all sticky!

MRS. PIPER: (*Tickling and cuddling him.*) Oh, sticky is it? Sticky-icky-wicky ... Pretty Pierre's fancy is all sticky-wicky ...

PERCY: Pierre?! God help me, what next?! (*Now taking a different tack.*) Mrs. Piper – er – I mean, I think your iris has been out of water a little too long – see, it's all droopy.

MRS. PIPER: (*Gazing down at the flower in her lapel.*) Oh, it is. (*Plucks up the iris.*) Poor little Iris, how she's suffered, being out in this terrible heat all day ...

PERCY: Maybe if you take her for a powder she'll freshen up?!

MRS. PIPER: Oh, I don't know, she looks in a bad way. It's a good thing we're here at the hospital. I'm sure someone here can revive her. Who do you think we should talk to?
(*She glances about, again fusses over the flower.*)

ACT TWO

Poor little Iris, all droopy ...

PERCY: I'm sure Dr. Lustig will have an answer ...

MRS. PIPER: I don't know. Oh Pierre, I think she's taken a turn for the worse.

PERCY: Can't be – she was fine – well, nearly fine – just a second ago.

MRS. PIPER: (*Panicking.*) No, no, she's much worse now!

PERCY: We'll get Nurse Lathrop, she'll find the doctor –

(*He attempts to rise but she restrains him.*)

MRS. PIPER: You're not going to leave me, not now, not with little Iris in the condition she's in ... How could you?!

PERCY: Well, I don't know, I just thought ...

(*A long moment passes.*)

MRS. PIPER: Oh my, I think she's coming round ... Look, look Pierre, she is, she's coming round!

PERCY: What a relief.

MRS. PIPER: Do you like my perfume?

PERCY: What?

MRS. PIPER: I was just wondering out-loud if you liked my perfume ...
(*She sniffs her wrist, then presses it close to PERCY's nose. He dutifully sniffs.*)

PERCY LIFAR

PERCY: Nice.

MRS. PIPER: It is, isn't it ... (*Again sniffs her wrist.*) Fragrance de Soleil du Music-Hall.

PERCY: Oh.

MRS. PIPER: (*Blushing.*) That's what I call it anyway. Want to know a secret? It's just plain eau de toilet. But I think it's quite nice, don't you, Pierre?

(*Again the wrist under his nose.*)

PERCY: (*Having had enough.*) Mrs. Piper, this place is no joke you know. It's in here that we suffer for the world-at-large!

MRS. PIPER: (*With childish sarcasm.*) Really, for the world-at-large? Let me feel your muscles then!

PERCY: I haven't any.

MRS. PIPER: Haven't any muscles?! How can this be when you suffer so?! I thought all great men who suffer – well – well – well, take Hercules, take Atlas, take Popeye!

(*She's left* PERCY *befuddled and irritated.*)

PERCY: Did you know, Mrs. Piper, that they stuff a rubber pad between the teeth when they give you the works?

MRS. PIPER: (*Sighs with feigned boredom.*) **The works**, is it terrible?

PERCY: (*With cold hostility.*) Yes, Mrs. Piper, **the works**. Aren't you curious to know what **the works** entail?

MRS. PIPER: Mildly.

ACT TWO

PERCY: It's fear makes you sweat, Mrs. Piper, Fear.

MRS. PIPER: Oh, I know that. I know that much.

PERCY: Good. Di you also know that animal's sweat through their noses? Well, they do. I read it in a magazine in the solarium. But that's how you're made to feel, like an animal, like an animal that's being lead to slaughter. Because you don't know how bad it's going to be each time ...

(*She's captivated and now oozes sincerity.*)

MRS. PIPER: I can't imagine anything like that. Are you sure?

PERCY: Believe me, this is the truth – I know.

(*But he's lying.*)

There you are like a hunted animal – trapped at the edge of a melting cliff, in the basement of a burning building, in the shallows of a boiling swamp – and there they are, waiting for you to make the wrong move, waiting to lower you inch by inch into the icy vat. It's a galvanized tub really, with a wire running from it to an electrical transformer – on rubber wheels, so nobody gets hurt. Once in the tub, gaunt reality succumbs to numbing cold. Vaporous images rise before the blackout curtains – aided by the medication administered beforehand – vaporous images more real than the most real dream, more real than reality itself – images decimating all reasoning as they rise – before the blackout curtains!

MRS. PIPER: My goodness.

PERCY: And do you know where these diabolical images come from, Mrs. Piper?

PERCY LIFAR

MRS. PIPER: (*Fluttering*.) Please, Mr. Lifar, you're frightening me ...

PERCY: That may be, but it's for a good cause!

MRS. PIPER: Well, alright then. No, I can't say I do know where these – ?

PERCY: Diabolical.

MRS. PIPER: These diabolical images come from.

PERCY: Goddamnit, lady, **your past**!

MRS. PIPER: I'm what?!

PERCY: Your past! These diabolical images come from your past – they stick you in a tub of iced water with an electrical wire shoved up your rectum, turn on the juice, and – hey, gadzooks – your bloody brain splatters these diabolical images all over their blackout curtains!

(MRS. PIPER *passes out*.)

Mind you, that's not the end of it though ...

(*He jerks to his feet and begins pacing before her inert figure, however addressing her as if she were still conscious.*)

There you are, the iced water lapping at the rim, your bones stuttering in their joints. Your thorax rises in a vast convulsion up out of the water. Like a tidal wave the iced water washes over the rim and onto the floor – thank goodness for those rubber wheels on the electrical transformer! A Nordic sea overflows about you, a promontory sea. And this promontory sea – yes, Nordic sea – gushes onto the plain below. Many

ACT TWO

people are drowned! But you are guiltless, being nature itself, and so their cries, the sound of their little boats cracking under the weight of the heaving iced water mean nothing. Your eyes pop open and what do you see, Mrs. Piper? Why, you see the massive bars on the windows burning like white-hot ingots through the blackout curtains. And there's no relief from these wicked stripes! Of course, of course, cast the gaze inward – it's all for nought: there's no relief in that darkness that lies within the skull, not relief at all, because there is no darkness, no darkness any longer, only diabolical images – images behind bars where they belong! Where they belong, I tell you, Mrs. Piper, where they belong. And there is no darkness any longer – no blessed darkness any longer, Mrs. Piper – imagine that!

(Exhausted, he sits, takes up MRS. PIPER's *limp hand. He caresses it. On the edge of this scene now stands* DR. LUSTIG *with another patient,* MR. PIPER.*)*

DR. LUSTIG: Lifar, what are you doing with Piper's wife? (*To* MR. PIPER.) Rather an affectionate chap, Lifar. But perfectly harmless. Believe me, sir, Lifar has only the best intentions.

Darkness.

SCENE 2

In the space that is the shaftway has been set a row of urinals. PERCY *stands at one, urinating. He speaks to his invisible listener, and turns his head to glance over his shoulder when wanting to make a particular point.*

PERCY: The droplets dripped ... one, two, three, and now ... four ... from the tip of my very own penis. And the urinals trickled disconsolately their once pristine chromium spigots clotted with hardening greenish slime. How marvellously observant we've become in our old age. And objective, one hopes. (*Turns, buttoning his fly.*) Ah but the disconsolate trickling, how it rings in the ears with sacrificial echo … and against the frosted, wire- re-enforced windows the pigeons' shadows play like a hundred children's hands. Yes, the sooty pigeons.

(*These shadows now play against the wall above him.*)

Now the pigeons rain heavenward and the frosted windows are again immutable, like fresh bars of soap!

(*And the shadows rise and are gone, leaving* PERCY *to gaze at the empty wall.*)

A window-shade perhaps, vapid and pale with late April light. But what April light reaches us here, from Tyrone's lonely shaftway? Not much, methinks.

(*After a moment, he traverses the set to mount the lobby staircase, arriving lastly on the balcony, where he again addresses the invisible listener.*)

It was cold on the terrace. I was shivering. The clinic's facade rose like a dirty yellow tornado behind me where I sat. (*Sits.*) My attention was drawn downward, to the entrance pavement, which was still stained with that morning's showers, and I watched as a man and a woman walked toward the gates. The man moved purposefully ahead and the woman fell back, as if the moment asked that her movements coincide with the slowness of her thoughts. At the gates, the man waited for the woman. He put his arm round her waist and held her face close to his. But she turned her cheek away and rested her head on his shoulder. When they passed through the gates the wind lifted their coats and the woman reached up to keep her hat from blowing away.

ACT TWO

(DR. LUSTIG *has come to stand beside* PERCY. *He too watches as the couple departs. Their attention lingers on the two. Now* DR. LUSTIG *regards* PERCY.)

DR. LUSTIG: How do you like your new robe?

PERCY: It's fine, but I keep wondering who wore it last. I have a feeling it was an old man. I have a feeling he died wearing it.

DR. LUSTIG: It's a perfectly good robe.

PERCY: I was wondering if you could get me some shoes. I'm no longer a medical patient, am I?

DR. LUSTIG: I don't know why they haven't given you any shoes. We'll take care of that straight away.

(*He sits by* PERCY, *again gazes from the balcony at the departing couple.*)

What do you make of them?

PERCY: I don't make anything of them. Do I?

DR. LUSTIG: Well, you did make something of the birds in the tree, and the clouds.

PERCY: Oh, that.

DR. LUSTIG: Yes, that. We've got to learn to do the same with people – got to learn to imbue them with our own meaning.

PERCY: 'Imbue' them?

DR. LUSTIG: Yes, **imbue** them. Imbue, instil.

PERCY LIFAR

PERCY: Ah yes, instil. As Mrs. Piper imbued young Percy with meaning ...

DR. LUSTIG: That's it. (*Laughs.*) Very clever, Percy.

PERCY: (*Referring to the couple just outside the gates.*) Those two, they're standing on the side of a steep mountain listening to the landslide that has begun a thousand yards above them. She's thinking of how she's squandered her life on artificial love, and he's thinking he wished he hadn't been possessed of a certain cruelty in the loins all his life.

DR. LUSTIG: 'A certain cruelty in the loins', I like that.

PERCY: Good. You see, now they attend their own hapless play. She feels the tarnished screw in the guts, he the broken plate of her cunt. Their routine is ended. No insult will provoke either's pride ever again.

(DR. LUSTIG *makes a note.*)

DR. LUSTIG: This is very complicated ...

PERCY: Not really. They are finished – for each other – their sad, crude poem cast upon the blazing heap, an inconsequential light, like the glinting head of a pin, there on the side of the mountain as we watch tons of earth and ice plummet towards them.

(DR. LUSTIG *peers at him, expecting more.*)

That is precisely what I see.

DR. LUSTIG: Of course the question is why? Why should you endow their apparent sadness – due perhaps to the hopeless

ACT TWO

condition of a loved one – with such intimate doom, such sexual desolation, in such terms? Why, do you think?

PERCY: You asked me what they meant to me, not what I imagine they are actually caught up in. It hasn't anything to do with me – what they're caught up in. I can build on the other, the landslide and that. How they got here I don't know, haven't the vaguest idea. And that's that. It's probably just as banal as their choice of words at this very moment. There, doctor, look there ...

(*They both fix on the distant couple.*)

... their deteriorating bodies hidden beneath their stiff, dark clothes, that bleak, forbidding street with its unnatural currents pulling them this way and that. What an utterly useless moment.

DR. LUSTIG: But how do we know that?

PERCY: I know.

DR. LUSTIG: No one can say you don't have confidence in your own interpretive capacities –

PERCY: You see, I can follow them down the street and into their two different worlds. In my imagination their world is divided. If they're suffering now, it's for the best. For the best in the scheme of things I imagine for them.

DR. LUSTIG: And what about the landslide?

PERCY: Oh, the landslide. The landslide never reaches them. It was never meant to.

DR. LUSTIG: If I read you correctly, the landslide is something akin to their anticipation ...

PERCY: Nothing more, nothing less. It only compels them to move a little quicker. You'll see, they'll move a little quicker now, now that they're getting farther and farther away from the gate.

(*DR. LUSTIG ponders this.*)

DR. LUSTIG: Well then, now that they're divided, what will become of them? What will become of them individually?

PERCY: Forgive me, doctor, but you weren't following me. They're only divided in this moment, in that moment. That moment is passed. You see, they're walking arm-in-arm now, and thankful for it!

DR. LUSTIG: But in your imagination they **are** divided ...

PERCY: Yes ... they are. But they don't know that.

DR. LUSTIG: And what they don't know can't hurt them ...

PERCY: Precisely. Dr. Lustig, you've grasped the self-perpetuating logic of this particular vision!

DR. LUSTIG: I really wish, Percy, that you would desist from patronizing – me, or anyone else. It does put people off, you know.

PERCY: But I wasn't. I am truly delighted – I mean, that you've grasped this one.

DR. LUSTIG: (*with consternation.*) There, you see –

ACT TWO

PERCY: Truly, I am.

(*But* DR. LUSTIG *won't be convinced of* PERCY's *sincerity.*)
I am.

DR. LUSTIG: (*Taking another note.*) Mr. & Mrs. Piper.

PERCY: What?

DR. LUSTIG: You mean, **who** ... Mr. & Mrs. Piper: the man and woman and the landslide.

PERCY: Oh, so that's Mrs. Piper again?

DR. LUSTIG: And Mr. Piper. He's been released in her care. It's been a long and arduous road but it seems he's recovered sufficiently. So, you see, Percy ...

PERCY: Well, at least now my baby won't be raised in a broken home.

DR. LUSTIG: (*Not comprehending.*) Your speaking in riddles again, or is that one of your obscure jokes?

PERCY: Not one of my jokes, doctor. But won't Mr. Piper be surprised in several months to find Mrs. Piper at her age dandling an invisible baby on her knee.

DR. LUSTIG: 'Invisible' is right.

PERCY: That's what I said, invisible.

(*Below them,* NURSE LATHROP *and* SISTER DANZELL *wheel* MISS EZRAD *in her 'recliner' over the lawn, up the entrance pavement, and into the lobby.* MISS EZRAD *is a rather pretty girl in her*

mid to late twenties who is however unnaturally thin and wan.
PERCY *and* DR. LUSTIG *observe their arrival.* NURSE
LATHROP *and* SISTER DANZELL *refer to* MISS EZRAD
as if she weren't there.)

LATHROP: (*Referring to* MISS EZRAD.) What a pity ...

DANZELL: And such lovely, sad eyes.

LATHROP: Sad, sad eyes.

DANZELL: And don't they just peer into one's soul.

LATHROP: That they do. (*Pauses to light a cigarette.*) A shroud of melancholy dust goes with her.

DANZELL: Indeed it does. (*Lights a cigarette of her own.*)

LATHROP: Something deathly in the air, one might say.

DANZELL: Indeed one might. Best to keep one's nose well out of it.

LATHROP: It does tend to break the resolve.

DANZELL: Indeed it does. Mildewed and decrepit, and at such a young age. What a pity ...

LATHROP: And such lovely, sad eyes.

DANZELL: Sad, sad eyes.

LATHROP: And don't they just peer into one's soul.

DANZELL: That they do ...

ACT TWO

(*As they pass through the lobby their voices become less distinct, as do their figures in the deepening gloom.*)

PERCY: (*Referring to* MISS EZRAD.) She's a fine, fine nose, like a solitary blade of grass.

DR. LUSTIG: And meatless cheeks. A grievous sight. Starving herself to death, I'm afraid. She keeps pulling the I.V. out with her teeth. (*Gazes into the sky.*) What a lovely bright day.

PERCY: (*Still dwelling on* MISS EZRAD's *plight.*) Why don't they put a tube down her throat and pump the gruel into her belly that way?

DR. LUSTIG: She's much too frail for that now. Golly, look how that plane is just trimming the clouds! I once had a plane very like that – when I was a boy – it was all silvery and sparkly too, with a blue propeller. Golly ...

PERCY: Beautiful. (*Remembering* MISS EZRAD *in her 'recliner'.*) Yes, very beautiful. Like she'd once worn a gardenia in her hair ...

DR. LUSTIG: Miss Ezrad – a gardenia in her hair?

PERCY: A white gardenia. A gardenia, Dr. Lustig.

DR. LUSTIG: Yes, I know. I know what a gardenia is.

PERCY: Like a token of things to come, of rooms whiter than white and colder than ice .. orderlies listening outside her door for the sound of her teeth tearing at her own death. Like that, doctor? You see, Miss Ezrad is good for me.

DR. LUSTIG: Maybe so, but she's not very good for herself.

PERCY: How heavenly her life must have been then, when she'd lain in her little bed, her mother and father sleeping soundly below, admiring her gardenia standing in its glass before the moon, its lush odour lulling her to sleep with evocations of an undreamt world.

DR. LUSTIG: I'd rather have been left out of it – her undreamt world. And that's a sacrilege for any doctor to say.

PERCY: Jesus, that bad, eh? Maybe I could have a word with her ...

DR. LUSTIG: (*Gazing dolefully at* PERCY.) I'm afraid she's stopped talking too. Stopped talking altogether. She's a young woman.

PERCY: That means just as much to me as it does to you.

DR. LUSTIG: (*Regarding* PERCY *more thoughtfully now.*) Maybe it does. In fact, Lifar, I'm sure it does. But there's really nothing to be gained from it, for you, I'm afraid.

PERCY: Oh, that doesn't matter – if you're concerned about my education – I get enough of that sort of thing from Vera and Ray.

DR. LUSTIG: Percy, you've only visited with them twice.

PERCY: Twice is enough.

(DR. LUSTIG, *now preoccupied with* MISS EZRAD *himself, begins worrying out-loud.*)

DR. LUSTIG: ... consumed by thought. Never any childhood to speak of, only thought. Young, then growing old very quickly, thinking. And now wanting to die on top of it. Her thoughts are finishing her off. The fatherly regret shows, doesn't it! (*Snaps out of it.*) Miss Ezrad is impossible! Percy, let me put it to you

ACT TWO

very simply – perhaps I shouldn't be telling you all this. Nonsense, it'll do me good to get it off my chest! (*Organises His thoughts.*) Percy, you see, everyone wants – and needs – to have someone, someone for himself along ... someone to remain as a child with, if you will. Miss Ezrad is the exception. Miss Ezrad alone is without this longing.

(PERCY *finds this hard to believe.*)

Well, I mean, she isn't the only one, but she is a hard case – the hardest case I've ever come across. In most people – unrealistic and, in a word, cowardly as this longing may be, it does serve a purpose. Distraction is the name of the game here, I think ... (*Referring to* Miss EZRAD's *case.*) Hopeless, confoundingly hopeless. And now, next to death.

PERCY: But not fragile. And hardly cowardly.

DR. LUSTIG: Maybe not. Maybe she does have beliefs of some kind.

PERCY: I imagine so.

DR. LUSTIG: Ah well, Percy, maybe it's not such a bad idea after all. Maybe you and she will hit if off! How? – I don't know.

PERCY: Especially if she isn't ... well, you know.

DR. LUSTIG: One never knows, maybe you can loosen her tongue.

PERCY: Maybe, you never know.

DR. LUSTIG: No, one never knows with an experiment such as this. One never knows.

PERCY: No, I guess not.

DR. LUSTIG: No, one never knows! Now, how about a game of croquet with Vice-Admiral Lillingston?!

Darkness.

SCENE 3

Evening. The nightshift has arrived and the dayshift is preparing to go home. NURSE LATHROP *and* SISTER DANZELL *are in the lobby putting on their coats and hats. The lobby has a sombre yellowish incandescence to it which foretells a long night.*

DANZELL: Those dreadful people were here again today.

LATHROP: They were, weren't they.

DANZELL: It always ends badly, doesn't it.

LATHROP: Indeed it does, Sister Danzell. Indeed it does. Oh damn, I've torn the lining! I've really got to slim.

DANZELL: But you've a lovely figure, Lathrop, just lovely.

LATHROP: You're much too kind, Danzell. Actually I don't have a very nice figure – if you compare it with those skinny little things you see running round everywhere today – but I suppose it may still suit in a classical sense.

DANZELL: Oh, I think so. Yes, that's what it is – classical.

LATHROP: Thank you, Danzell. But you really are much too kind. (*Plumps her coat over her hips and reaches down with some effort for her hat which waits on the chair.*) Hmmph ... (*Referring to the hat.*) Come here now, you tricky little bugger ...

(*As she fixes her hat on her head, she glances at* DANZELL's.)

ACT TWO

That's nice.

DANZELL: What? Oh, oh this old thing. I've had this ages. You've seen this before.

LATHROP: Have I? No, Sister Danzell, I don't think I have. You know, you really do have such pretty things ... (*Reaches out to lay her hand on* SISTER DANZELL's *breast.*)

DANZELL: (*Arms akimbo.*) Oh my ... when you do that I just want to – to do something wicked! To prance and cavort, Lathrop, to prance and cavort ...

LATHROP: (*Considering the bulge beneath her hand.*) What beautiful stitching. It's just lovely, you know, Danzell, just lovely ... (*Snapping out of her fevered-trance.*) You were on Lifar's floor today, weren't you?

DANZELL: (*Snapping out of her own.*) Yes, I was.

LATHROP: And what was the upshot? I mean, with those dreadful people ...

DANZELL: Well, it ended badly. It really did, it just ended badly.

LATHROP: But what actually happened? Did Lifar urinate on the woman's purse, as before?

DANZELL: No, I don't think he did – no signs of urination.

LATHROP: No.

(*They slowly make their way across the lobby and exit the building. Once outside, they linger on the pavement, the chill rising about them.*)

DANZELL: No, none of that this time. I only have it second-hand though – from Lifar himself – which means there is embroidery.

LATHROP: (*Laughs.*) Yes, there would be, wouldn't there, Sister Danzell?!

DANZELL: I'm afraid so. It was priceless ...

(SISTER DANZELL *giggles gleefully.*)

LATHROP: Was it now?

DANZELL: Oh, it was, it was, Nurse Lathrop! And the way he told it – like it meant the world to him to get it right!

LATHROP: He really is such a dear.

DANZELL: (*Begins pacing and gesticulating as Percy does when addressing his invisible listener.*) He said Vera'd begun picking through his hair like a mama chimp – looking for vermin, he thought. And of course we keep him extremely clean, so I resented the implication.

LATHROP: I would have as well.

DANZELL: Vera then noticed that his hair was turning white – which I haven't noticed – have you?

LATHROP: I don't know why I should.

DANZELL: Vera then told him that his white hair would give him an air of distinction when his terrible ordeal was over and he was back on civvy street ---

ACT TWO

LATHROP: Imagine that – 'civvy street' – you'd think there was a war going on or something!

DANZELL: Well, exactly. Lifar begged off, as usual, saying the end to his ordeal was a long way off, if such things ever ended.

LATHROP: I hate to see such pessimism in a patient.

DANZELL: Well so do I. So do I. He said that righteous indignation just steamed from her eyes and then she began tugging on his forelock – with a vengeance. Tears burst from her eyes and her husband – Ray, I think he's called – had to restrain her.

LATHROP: Same as before.

DANZELL: Nearly identical.

(NURSE LATHROP *shakes her head sadly and the two nurses walk off, into the night. A light goes on in Percy's room, where he is sitting on his bed, relaxing. He continues* Sister Danzell's *account of Vera and Ray's visit.*)

PERCY: The colourful clowns and picaroons on Vera's smock were besmirched with her copiously flowing tears. The cheap dye ran in floral confluences, and the big-mouthed faces of the clowns and picaroons themselves became like flowers. Gay **and** grotesque, they were, delightfully so. Eventually the clown and picaroon flowers melted into purple streams and bled over Vera's heaving bosom – to the dam-breast of her bodice – and fell, like April showers, into her lap, where the purple lay like a piece of liver. Thusly, Vera expired – her tears in her lap, a false breath of Spring in the air. She'd at last attained a state of spiritual grace. Her countenance was one of glowing passivity. The facial reliquary Ray held aloft in his great powdery hands positively beamed contentment. Yes, at long last Vera had found silence, and so had we all. And what a relief it was, this

heavenly silence of Vera's. 'Ah so ...' This and only this did I
hear the forbearing Ray murmur as he carried her from the
room. Hushed too were the benighted cries I'd heard tearing
at my own breast. All the world was wonderfully, wonderfully
silent. An illusion of life had vanished from my room, and in
its place had come life itself, serene and still in its occupation.
My room was once again alive with my own thoughts, filled
to brimming with my – oh, you darling sweet man – with my
very own thoughts. And I was consumed with keen anticipation as Miss Ezrad's own thinking-presence rose before me,
like a tree. 'But what meaning – for Vera and Ray – have **you**?'
her presence asked. 'What meaning have you?' And, you
know, I didn't know. 'They shall drink from you as from a
broken vessel, forever,' cautioned Miss Ezrad, 'always thirsting.
Unless, that is, you allow them a glimpse of what never was
and never shall be: a glimpse of the sweet perfection by which
they are enslaved, a glimpse of your own sweet self atop the
pillar of their dreaming, a glimpse to end their blindness, to
absolve them of the terrible guilt they feel having wrought
you – according to them – and delivered you into this terrible
world. A glimpse, Percy, to explode the grain of a future once
glimpsed as it floated upon the blinding haze of their youth!'
And, with that, I'd burst into tears myself, and wept with joy,
as I'd seen, through Miss Ezrad, who I'd never actually met, a
way to heal their desolate lives, a way to actually get Vera and
Ray off my back for good! 'Thank you, Miss Ezrad!' I cried,
and meant it.

(*He takes a moment to absorb the shock of this emotional outpouring,
then smiles with radiant amusement, which for* PERCY *is happiness.*
TYRONE *bellows at the bottom of the shaftway, and is illuminated.*)

TYRONE: God help me!

(PERCY *gapes at the open window.*)

ACT TWO

God help me!

(TYRONE *gazes longingly at the empty wall, conjuring an imaginary cruciform. As* PERCY *creeps to the window, the silver cord upon which he will be lowered to meet* TYRONE *descends. He grasps the cord and is lowered down.* TYRONE's *gaze remains fixed on the wall, his wide back to* PERCY.)

How exalted, my wall. How exalted, with her fine face tilted heavenward. Good Lord, how exalted ...

(*He glances from the wall to the ground below. He kneels to touch the grass.* PERCY *goes quietly to him and, not wanting to surprise him, places his hand gently on* TYRONE's *shoulder.*)

PERCY: Fair warning, Tyrone.

(TYRONE *turns to smile up at him.* PERCY *touches his forefinger to his lips, asking* TYRONE *to remain silent.*)

Let's say that all our days here are only a brief interlude. Let's say that all these white angles, steaming dishes, electrical fences, and damp nettle-beds pass away, as things do outside. And let's say that you and I and – well, take Miss Ezrad for instance – let's say we all survive, survive pretty much unscathed, even emboldened. If we were to say all that, Tyrone – which is saying a lot – how would you recommend we enter or re-enter the world-at-large?

(*Pondering this,* TYRONE *rises to his feet.*)

Not by the main gate?

TYRONE: Firstly, Mr. Lifar, if you were to be excused by the main gate, they'd never stop watching you. I believe they'd give you over to others like themselves.

PERCY LIFAR

PERCY: Highly-strung animals, you mean.

TYRONE: You could put it that way. I would prefer the terminology **intelligences**, or **minor intelligences** – outside, **minor intelligence**. Any way you slice it, we are their playthings. Frankly, sir, they know. Their livelihoods depend on knowing.

PERCY: Know what?

TYRONE: What each of us is all about. Everything. I believe they take the info straight out through the eyes and record it on millions of tiny notepads they have stuck in their heads. It hurts me to have to tell you this, but I don't think there is any getting out of here. Out there is still in here, if you follow. And so, Mr. Lifar, not wanting to contradict myself – because that would be lying in a fashion and close to sin – I am, in a manner of speaking, content. My only goal in this life is to atone for my sins. I figure I've got just as good a chance at atonement in here as out there.

(*With that,* TYRONE *stretches and kneads the night air with his big hands.*)

God help me!

(*Having bellowed thusly, he curls back to his normal size.*)

PERCY: There's something else I'd like to ask you about, Tyrone, of a more personal nature ...

TYRONE: It's nothing dirty I hope? I just shut my ears to that filthy talk – like we get in the kitchen.

PERCY: No, it's nothing dirty. It's about Miss Ezrad, who's more or less in the same boat.

ACT TWO

TYRONE: Miss Ezrad? – I don't believe I've had the pleasure.

PERCY: I can tell you, the pleasure would be a little frightening: you see, she's starving herself to death.

TYRONE: Oh that young lady. She's not starving herself to death, she's been that thin and scrawny for years.

PERCY: But don't you think she's beautiful? Why she's ageless.

TYRONE: Aged, if you were to ask me.

PERCY: Actually, she's very young, or so I've been told. Dr. Lustig has agreed that she and I are to comprise an experiment. An experiment, that's how he sees it. Miss Ezrad and I are to comrise an experiment in the various forms of communication, or lack thereof.

TYRONE: Sounds beastly.

PERCY: Hopefully, Miss Ezrad and I can unscramble all the subliminal signals we're each giving out. We would then actually converse, using words, while moving, simultaneously, through space. I say we can.

TYRONE: An experiment ... ?

(*His brow furrows.*)

Beastly and tricky ...

PERCY: (*Growing agitated.*) No, I don't think so, not for me. Living minds, Tyrone, hers and mine: deflected – granted, largely taciturn – it's true, but still sound-sparking organs wanting to take flight! Dr. Lustig would perhaps disagree ...

PERCY LIFAR

TYRONE: Maybe he would, maybe he wouldn't.

PERCY: Whatever. Mental textures to be observed, and manipulated, at a remove, at various intervals, because of, rather than in spite of, their peculiarity, by Dr. Lustig ...

TYRONE: The string-puller of all time.

PERCY: I know, it sounds sinister. Maybe it is. The real fly in the ointment – well, I proposed this experiment, inadvertently. Me. Yes, Tyrone, this experiment, or the format by which it shall be known as such. And for no apparent reason. Certainly without purpose. Absolutely none. No reason, no purpose: what's the sense in it? This, I ask myself. In lacking motive, do I remain safe? Not likely ...
(TYRONE *shakes his head 'no'.*)

It isn't very likely, you agree. There are always repercussions, aren't there ... Someone – in this case Dr. Lustig – always managed to make something out of it. Some reason for each action and, of course, word. Can we, Tyrone, Miss Ezrad and I, outsmart them? Or is even the contemplation of such outsmarting playing into their hands? His hands, anyway?

(TYRONE *takes a long time thinking this over. He gazes up at the empty wall, then at* PERCY, *then at the wall.*)

TYRONE: Folly.

(*But* PERCY *hasn't heard him properly and another long pause follows.*)

Folly.

(TYRONE, *having gotten his message across, goes to sit with his back against the wall. Immobile, he regards* PERCY, *who turns to*

ACT TWO

the audience, again his invisible listener.)

PERCY: I knew Tyrone was right: it was folly. Would I always fall prey to such ridiculous spontaneity on the part of my mindless self? Was this response to the emaciated creature they called Miss Ezrad nothing more than impulsiveness on my part? I thought on, Tyrone thinking right along with me, and a number of rather ponderous terms plunked head-first onto the conveyor-belt: objectification of the rarefied self, poetically prompted superimposition, vicarious verification of the qualitative sensibility, isolated ectoplasmic transfer, etc. None of which – science be damned – captured the immediacy of what I'd felt as my eyes had fallen – grotesque image, that – had fallen on Miss Ezrad. Why, somewhere at that very moment in that vast labyrinth of impervious observers she went spinning, dusting the pathways with the ashes of her fallen contemporaries, each fallen in the shadow of some worthless statue. The temptation is to speak of love, but such an abstraction freezes the tongue – yet another grotesque image. But this throbbing heart of mine is itself grotesque, I fear! Or is it?!

TYRONE: *(Shaking his head woefully.)* In the spring they meet under the pines, deep in the woods behind. And sometimes their union results in what you might call a marriage – why, there might even be a baby or two. Mr. Lifar, it's frowned upon – that is unless engineered by the doctors. And woe be unto the dreamers who think they can carry on loving forever. I've seen it, what can happen if you get in too deep with another patient ... Believe me, you can wind up in a pretty sorry mess. I've been there, my friend. I've been there – and believe me, I'm still paying for it.

PERCY: But you're a trustee now. And you seem fairly contented.

TYRONE: Oh Lord, **contented**, it's a fine word, but it doesn't hold any water with me. No – forgive me, Lord – I am not contented.

PERCY: If only the River Jordan were nearby.

TYRONE: Yes sir, if only. But it ain't. And what's up here – (*Taps his head.*) – well, I know how it got there, and you know too.

PERCY: Yes, I do. I do know. Electronics.

TYRONE: Bless you, sir. Then you know: I am damned. You know it, and I know it. Let's make no bones about it – damned.

(*Too tired to leap clawing at the sky, he remains slumped there, and his cry is hollow and weak.*)

God help me!

Fade out.

SCENE 4

Dawn. MISS EZRAD *stands alone on the balcony like a figurine on the bow of a ship, her breasts thrust into the breeze, her hands planted firmly on the parapet. It is a shock to see her standing. She addresses the rising sun.*

MISS EZRAD: (*Taking a deep breath.*) What fragrance! Is it the lilac yonder, beyond that grey wall? The honeysuckle curling over it? Or is it the new mown grass, the buds of clover scattered and ripening in the dew? You there! You, blushing light, hidden in your bed below the horizon, what do you make of all these sweet smells? Arise, tell me! This is my day – do you hear?! My day!

And what a good day it is!

ACT TWO

(*Again she breathes deeply, runs her hands sensuously through her hair, and, eyes closed, basks in the balmy mists. When she addresses the sun again, it is in a confessional tone.*)

He came to me again in my dreams last night, my Raphael. It's a beautiful name, Raphael, especially when spoken with a passionate Spanish accent. Raphael and I walked hand-in-hand along the corridors, to the solarium. The moonlight streamed across the carpet – what beautiful feet he has, like a swimmer's. He took me into an empty room – carried me as if I were his bride – and lay me on the bed, and lay his head in my lap. And there it rested – Raphael's sleek Spanish head. How profoundly endearing it was. He fell asleep that way, with his head in my lap. But first he asked me to tell him a story. You know, I thought and thought and the only one I could think of was about the time I worked for Mr. Florescu, at his shop by the hotel. It was a summer job for me – I was only twelve. I think Raphael liked that, that I was only twelve, because it told him something about how I used to be, before I took ill. I told him about the screen I was restoring – a painted, oriental one. I tried to describe the tiny figures for him – he must have been asleep but it didn't matter because I was so fascinated by what I saw on the screen before me. The scenes meandered lazily over the screen. The tiny figures were running for cover, some already glowing with the wave of heat that was sweeping over them. When I looked closer I could see that some of them had already been fixed by the heat. I could feel the warmth of Raphael's saliva dampening my leg as he slept. Then there was someone standing behind me, listening. I knew it wasn't Mr. Florescu.

(*It is* DR. LUSTIG. *Startled,* MISS EZRAD *turns.*)

DR. LUSTIG: Sorry, Miss Ezrad, but we hear you speak so seldom, and you do have such a lovely voice.

(*She says nothing and turns away, her hands covering her face.*)

PERCY LIFAR

Asthma-weather – what a chaff-ridden wind – here, have my handkerchief.

(*But she won't take it.*)

There's someone here who'd like to have a word with you. You'll see, I think you and Mr. Lifar – you and Percy – will have lots to talk about. I'm sure the two of you will get on very well. Give it a chance, Helen ...

(PERCY *waits in the lobby.* DR. LUSTIG *pats* MISS EZRAD *on the shoulder, to reassure her, and leaves to get* PERCY. MISS EZRAD *turns to address the now blazing morning sun.*)

MISS EZRAD: What could I possibly have to say to this man?

(DR. LUSTIG *finds* PERCY *staring at the overhead light in the lobby in a benumbed state of apprehension.*)

DR. LUSTIG: Never fear, her bark is worse than her bite ... (*Laughs good-naturedly.*) I have a tip for you – something that just came up – it may make the whole thing go a lot easier.

(*He waits to see if* PERCY *is listening; he is.*)

Ask her about the screen, the oriental screen she restored for Mr. Florescu when she was twelve.

PERCY: For who?

DR. LUSTIG: For Mr. Florescu. Got it?
PERCY: I think so.

DR. LUSTIG: OK, let's go.

ACT TWO

(They cross the lobby and mount the steps leading to the hallway above and to the balcony. As they go, MISS EZRAD pleads with her god, the sun, to save her from this meeting.)

MISS EZRAD: Whatever I've done to deserve this, I didn't mean to ... If it was dreaming of Raphael? Only I did. But I can't stop from dreaming. I can't. Oh, what have I done to deserve this ...

(PERCY and DR. LUSTIG appear at the door to the balcony. She refuses to acknowledge their entrance.)

DR. LUSTIG: If you need me just call – I'll be just there in the hall – reading Lathrop's minutes from the staff meeting.

(PERCY moves closer to MISS EZRAD, who automatically shies away. DR. LUSTIG watches them for a moment, then shakes his head with a certain irritation.)
Now, you two sit and talk! Sit!

(With wounded resign, they both sit. DR. LUSTIG smiles with satisfaction and departs. They sit in silence for a long, long moment, in their matching grey robes. PERCY finds being in her presence extremely moving. She feels this and looks at him. Naturally, he smiles at her. Miraculously, she returns his smile.)

PERCY: He told me to ask you about the screen.

MISS EZRAD: He was spying on me.

PERCY: I know. I'm sorry. He spies on me too.

(They both gaze out over the balcony.)

What's that, what's that aroma – it's like freshly mown hay. I don't know how I know that but I do.

PERCY LIFAR

MISS EZRAD: It may be the cut grass and clover – together. I smelled it earlier.

PERCY: It's lovely isn't it?

MISS EZRAD: Yes.

PERCY: I have amnesia. Sounds like a foreign country, doesn't it? Like I'm the king of some peculiar foreign country. Amnesia.

MISS EZRAD: I don't have that, I have something else.

PERCY: You don't have to tell me.

MISS EZRAD: I don't mind. It's **psychic masochism**. I suffered trauma when I was twelve. Usually people suffer it earlier, but mine came late. How did you come to suffer amnesia?

PERCY: There's not much suffering involved, I don't think. But then I don't know what happened to me either. Or I won't let on, that's what Dr. Lustig says. He says I just won't let on.

(*They both think these things over for a moment.*)

You were twelve when you restored that screen, that oriental screen for Mr. – ?

MISS EZRAD: Florescu. They tell me I never did restore that screen. They tell me it's only a metaphor – a kind of trick my mind is playing on me to keep me from knowing what actually happened. I don't mind telling you about the screen – if you really want to know.

PERCY: Only if you really want to tell me.

(*She thinks it over.*)

ACT TWO

MISS EZRAD: It's OK.

PERCY: OK.

MISS EZRAD: Mr. Florescu was a kind and gentle man. I was honoured. It was when I was restoring the screen that I realized that my happiness was just the most ephemeral thing. Not only was it intangible – just then – but it could vanish in a second, leaving me empty. I wasn't part of anything. Only my brush touching the screen anchored me to reality. Only my brush. My brush brought drop after drop of gold to tip the geishas' umbrellas and my being just bled out of me. The geishas smiled, and the watery sky above them grew brilliant with my gold, with what was coming out of me. I knew the screen would absorb me and there would be nothing left – just a hand holding a brush. As I feathered the white on, bringing the blossoms to life, all the poetry I imagined was waiting for me fluttered away, onto the screen. And the geishas smiled up at me. But their smiles were bitter, and empty. I lavished all the love I had on each scene: I knew how the geishas had died, drowned in a sea of fire. I longed for my own silence.

(*She has nothing more to say, and* PERCY *doesn't know what to say. A long moment passes.*)

PERCY: Has Mr. Florescu ever come – to visit you?

MISS EZRAD: No, I've never seen him again. He drank, I think. He may be dead now.

PERCY: I had a friend who may be dead now too. He was a famous violin player – you may have heard of him – his name was Oscar Bruno.

MISS EZRAD: No, I've never heard of him. But that doesn't mean much. I mean, I've been here so long.

PERCY: Me too. Whatever became of the screen?

MISS EZRAD: I don't know, if one accepts that it was real. I suppose Mr. Florescu sold it. The soldier who'd left it never came back.

PERCY: Oh.

(*He wants desperately to tell her about himself, but he hasn't anything to tell.*)

I have to apologize. You see, I don't know anything. A few people have told me things – like Oscar Bruno, and Vera and Ray, who claim to be my parents ... Oh, and Tyrone. Tyrone's a trustee. He does the dishes. But I think he's a lot crazier than me? I don't know for sure, but I think so. Vera and Ray are crazy too, but in a way that – well, that lets them stay outside.

MISS EZRAD: You don't seem very crazy to me. I don't think having amnesia is actually being crazy.

PERCY: Maybe not. I don't know. I can tell you what it's been like being here. (*Despairs.*) But then you already know what it's like being here.

MISS EZRAD: That's OK: I have my interpretation and you have yours.

PERCY: I guess that's one way of looking at it.

MISS EZRAD: So why not tell me?

PERCY: Alright. Bear with me though, I do have a tendency to embroider – but that's only because I really don't have anything to say.

ACT TWO

MISS EZRAD: That's alright.

PERCY: Well ...

(*But he doesn't know where to begin.*)

MISS EZRAD: (*Feeling sorry for him.*) How did you burn your hands?

PERCY: (*Stares down at them.*) I don't know.

(*A cloud of soot rolls over the balcony. It envelopes* MISS EZRAD *and* PERCY. *She rises, brushing at her face, the soot having gotten in her eyes.* PERCY *rises too, to help her.*)
It's coming from the boiler-room ... They're burning out the chimney ...

MISS EZRAD: They do that don't they ...

PERCY: It's awful.

MISS EZRAD: I know.

(*They hover together, their eyes shut tight against the black wind. She reaches out to grab hold of his robe to steady herself.* PERCY *takes her in his arms and holds her tightly, her face tucked under his. The black wind gusts about them.* DR. LUSTIG *watches with amusement from an upper window. With effort,* MISS EZRAD *and* PERCY *make their way into the building.*)

In the lobby, NURSE LATHROP *and* SISTER DANZELL *sit side-by-side, their white handkerchiefs pressed to their faces. But the wind abates and the soot quickly settles.* SISTER DANZELL, *who is doing the crossword, reaches up to turn on the standing-lamp beside her.*

DANZELL: What's kabuki, Nurse Lathrop?

LATHROP: What's what ... ?

DANZELL: **Kabuki** – what's kabuki? I think it may be the word I'm looking for.

LATHROP: Kabuki? How should I know?! (*Thinks for a moment.*) Sounds like a game. Some sort of foreign game.

DANZELL: It says here the players wear painted masks.

LATHROP: My educated guess would be it's a game – a game in ancient times most likely. Painted masks makes me think of the Incas – I believe they engaged in field sports. A rock or a ball or something was slung through the air with a kind of curvy stick. They'd have to have worn protective masks doing something like that. It may not have been the Incas but I would venture a guess it was some sort of South American tribe.

(SISTER DANZELL *accepts this mystifying definition good-naturedly.*)

Thank God. (*Referring to the settling of the soot which came from the burning out of the boiler-room chimney.*) I really wish they'd do that at night like they used to. It's that new governor ...

(SISTER DANZELL *counts the boxes for the word in question.*)

DANZELL: Oh my goodness, it's only three letters – it's too long anyway! Seventeen across. Another diabolical one ...

(*She reads the definition to herself, ponders it, then puts her newspaper down, lost in reverie.*)

Lathrop, have you ever longed to do something wild – I mean, really wild – like ride naked through the jungle on the back of a tiger?

ACT TWO

LATHROP: Christ no, Sister, why should I when I've got you?!
(*She laughs and laughs.*)

(NURSE LATHROP *and* SISTER DANZELL *continue sitting as the light dims.* VERA *and* RAY *enter the lobby and take seats.* MISS EZRAD *reclines in her wheelchair on the balcony.* DR. LUSTIG *peruses his notes slouched against a wall in the hallway.* PERCY *daydreams upon his bed. And* TYRONE *stands in the shaftway, gazing longingly at the empty wall. They are all softly illuminated.*)

The night sounds of the woodland behind the institution now emerge as the set is transformed into a bit of the garden: a stand of tall, whispering pines in silhouette against a dawning sky.

Coda

Coda

DR. LUSTIG *stands alone before the pines. He addresses the audience conversationally, almost as if he were casually confiding in a friend. Behind him are scattered various rusty and broken pieces of lawn furniture. A pitcher of water, glasses, and a victrola rest upon a table.*

DR. LUSTIG: Let's look at it the other way round: the clinic has provided them – all the imbeciles, mutes, frenetic, and fiends – with a captive audience of one: me. I know I'm wealthy in the numbers of whisperers and watchers I have stored inside, but you must also think of the pageantry that I've provided them. Why paint our cause here as anything but heroic? These are not paying guests, these are my guests, and I look after them in grand style. I keep them entertained. I wine and dine them, so to speak. I even tuck them in at night if need be. Of course we have our nasty techniques to deal with the unruly, but nothing so grim – nothing so grim as employment, taxation, or social security. No, my guests are the great adventurers of our age, of any age for that matter – they test the rope, sound the well, feel the mettle. No one here is allowed to lie in an enfeebled foetal pose for long, there's no faking oblivion within these four walls. Here, one is catapulted into a new reality. Here, the omnipresent gloom of the universe is vanished. Here, captivity is a kind of honourable paradise. For so many here the world outside was a numbing and unendurable place, a desolate place. Here we are safe from the desolate history of such a desolate place. Here we have ourselves to thank for our every pleasure, and the pleasures are manifold. And here, needless to say, no intruder intrudes.

(*He casts an affectionate glance over the grounds, sighs with satisfaction. He hears someone coming through the pines and turns to see who it is. It's* PERCY. DR. LUSTIG *turns back to briefly confide in the audience once more.*)

What wonders we've done with him ... He treats his parents, Vera and Ray, like royalty now; he's gotten up a poker game with Tyrone and the other dishwashers on a Monday evening; he carries on a friendly correspondence with Mrs. Piper – censored of course; why, he's even got Miss Ezrad eating and putting on a little weight. And all this in the blinking of an eye! (*Calls to* PERCY.) Percy, over here ... Can I have a word?

(PERCY *strolls over to* DR. LUSTIG.)

Hey, Perce, how are you and Miss Ezrad getting on?

(*He winks at the audience.*)

PERCY: Ineluctable.

DR. LUSTIG: Ah, **ineluctable**. That she is. No sense in struggling against a compelling personality like hers! Is there?!

PERCY: No, I guess not.

DR. LUSTIG: Speak of the devil – here she comes now. I'll leave you two to your own devices.

PERCY: Right. Thank you, doctor.

DR. LUSTIG: No – I thank you. You're a regular little miracle-worker, Perce.

PERCY: Thanks again.

DR. LUSTIG: Don't mention it.

(NURSE LATHROP *and* SISTER DANZELL *wheel* MISS EZRAD *into the shade, beside the table with the pitcher and glasses. They do a little business concerning the path the sun will take across the sky,*

CODA

then tuck her blanket more tightly around her and leave, arm-in-arm, whistling. PERCY *goes to sit by her.* DR. LUSTIG *ceases lingering now and he too leaves.* MISS EZRAD *and* PERCY *are alone at last. For a long moment they simply gaze quietly at one another.*)

PERCY: Your hair is surprisingly shiny for someone prone to malnutrition. It positively dazzles against the trees.

MISS EZRAD: But my cheeks ... you see ... (*Presses them in with her long thin fingers.*) ... they're much too lean.

PERCY: But they're blushing with colour! And your pupils are large as a cat's –

MISS EZRAD: And my lips are wet with expectancy!

(*They both laugh at the sauciness of this remark, coming at such an odd moment. Again they are quiet.*)

PERCY: Are you cold, shall we go inside?

MISS EZRAD: No, I have something I want to tell you. You've inspired me. I'm rewriting my life. I'm creating a new life for myself. It begins just as I described it to you the other day. You know, I was terribly frightened of meeting you, but now I know that our meeting had great significance. My faith is unshakable now. I don't know why, but it is.

PERCY: Maybe that's what I should do, instead of worrying.

MISS EZRAD: What's that?

(*But he doesn't answer.*)

What should you do?

PERCY: Maybe I should stop worrying and just make it up, like you're going to do.

MISS EZRAD: Why not? Nobody will ever know the difference.

PERCY: Maybe not. Do you really think so?

MISS EZRAD: No one ever knows anyway. They only know what they're told.

PERCY: Maybe you're right.

MISS EZRAD: That's what I'm going to do. And it's largely due to you.

(PERCY *thinks on this, but he's not convinced.*)

PERCY: But me ... My mind's been a blank for so long. How Would I ever begin? Tyrone bellowing in the night next door? Oscar clinging to me like a baby? Vera and Ray watching over me, thinking I'm asleep? Nurse Lathrop tearing the cotton from my eyes, but uncovering nothing? – no ancient profundities, no trampled pottery or dusty clues, no tattered maps, no gargoyles, no Dead Sea scrolls. You see, Miss Ezrad, this is all I know.

MISS EZRAD: But what would you want to say – look at it that way – I am. I'm going to set down just what I want. And you can do the same, whether you write it or talk it – it doesn't matter. Say what you want to say. Take your scarred hands, take the wound that's healed on your chest – it's up to you how these things happened. No one else knows. No one else can say. You can tell me anything you want and I'll believe you ... ?

(*Now he must say something. He closes his eyes and searches for something of meaning to say, a place to begin. He opens his eyes,*

CODA

looks into hers. For another long moment he is silent, thinking.)

PERCY: I knew my heart was beating, and it was the only sound I'd heard. It was just there, by itself, beating in my chest. And the sound of it was so great and so terrible that I was afraid. I became more and more afraid. And the more afraid I got the louder it got until my head was bursting with it. I felt the fire spreading from my heart into my veins. It crept slowly along my veins, driven by the beating. I touched my chest and felt its heat, I dug with my fingers into my chest to let it out but the fire reached out to grab me. And my hands stayed there, fastened to my flaming heart. And the fire burned, and my hands burned, and all the world turned black.

(MISS EZRAD gazes at him in wonderment. Anything she might say could only cast doubt upon the moment, so she says nothing.)

Do you believe me?

(Her expression communicates her belief. They sit in silence, thinking and listening, as the breeze whispers through the pines and the morn--ing sun shines harder.)

Would you like to hear a song, I could play a song on the victrola?

MISS EZRAD: That would be nice.

(He gets up and puts a record on. They listen for a while, then PERCY asks her to dance. With his help, she shakily rises and they dance among the pines.)

The song playing is 'Tenderly' by Gross and Lawrence, as sung by Billy Eckstine:

PERCY LIFAR

The evening breeze caressed the trees,
tenderly

The trembling trees embraced the breeze,
tenderly

Then you and I came wandering by and lost
in a sigh were we

The shore was kissed by sea and mist,
tenderly

I can't forget how two hearts met,
breathlessly

Your arms opened wide and closed me inside

You took my lips, you took my love,
tenderly

Curtain.